The Power Of Powerlessness

Powerful AA Step 1 Workbook & Journal

For 12 Step Fellowships With Six Week Journal & Trigger Tracker

First Step Prayer

Help me to see and admit that I am powerless over my alcoholism. Help me to understand how my alcoholism has led to unmanageability in my life. Help me this day to understand the true meaning of powerlessness. Remove from me all denial of my alcoholism. (developed from the chapter, More About Alcoholism)

The Power Of Powerlessness: Powerful AA Step 1 Workbook & Journal

First Printing, 2023

ISBN: 9798377098041

First Edition 2023

Disclaimer: Every reasonable effort has been made to ensure that the information provided in this book was correct at the time of publication. The author and publisher do not assume and hereby disclaim any responsibility and/or liability for any loss, damage, disruption, or adverse effects resulting from the use of the information found within this book, whether by errors, omissions, negligence, accident, or any other cause.

Books published by Imaginate Publishing are available at special discount rates for bulk purchases by corporations, institutions, and other organizations. For more information, please contact Imaginate Publishing at www.imaginateonline.com

From the Author:

Part of our journey is learning our misconceptions and how those have injured us, our relationships, our dreams, our potential. Not to mention steal our joy and, more importantly, our peace. Getting that back, or for the first time, is a painful road but one worth traveling. It begins with self-acceptance. Accepting all our parts-good, bad, and boring. To do that, we have to *SEE* those parts. Those things that we have disowned, denied, hidden out of our sight.

Understand this, you are not seeking to recover *FROM* anything, your seeking to recover (get back) that which you have lost, or, never got the chance to cultivate and develop in the first place. Like feeling good enough and fully accepted and loved *IN SPITE OF* your shortcomings rather than because of your good qualities.

It's going to be painful; it's going to be scary; you're going to struggle with guilt, you're going to fight the good fight with denial. As you work this step, remember that you are more than your addiction. You have flaws, you are human after all. Remember and accept your humanness.

I believe that you have the courage to go on this journey. Simply changing behavior is quite difficult as it goes against our grain. Change which comes from within will automatically change one's behavior because it changes the grain. Find the change your looking for from inside you, that's where it's been hiding all your life.

Love and peace to you,

Diana — not a coincidence.

First Step Prayer

Help me to see and admit that I am powerless over my alcoholism. Help me to understand how my alcoholism has led to unmanageability in my life. Help me this day to understand the true meaning of powerlessness. Remove from me all denial of my alcoholism. (developed from the chapter, More About Alcoholism)

Introduction

Congratulations on making the very difficult and scary decision to become sober. Maybe you lost someone important to you, or your health became pretty scary, or you lost everything you owned, or you hit a midlife crisis, or you're simply getting tired. Many of us have had to find our faces down in the dirt or have a major heart attack before we could even think of sobriety. For others, it was enough to see the direction we were heading. Whatever the reason, please give yourself credit for at least toying with the idea of sobriety.

Change can be quite frightening, especially when we are talking about completely giving up that which we believed soothed us in some form. I don't know about you but, for me, the very thought of not ever being able to use again was anxiety provoking.

To make things scarier, we know this kind of a change will also alter many of our relationships. We will lose some and have to fight to keep others. Even the people we know will stick around, we know the dynamics in those relationships will change. How do we prepare for this?

Sometimes we find ourselves on a journey we never expected to take. "*No way, not me!*" Maybe because we know, or assume, that road is a very difficult and painful one. Who wants that? But here we are, choosing it after all. Scary. But we're not alone, none of us are. If others before us traveled the same path and survived, and even thrived, so too can you and I. It's not impossible!

We should be sure that we have a counselor or sponsor before delving into Step One. That said, this workbook is intended to be worked on with a qualified sponsor, recovery specialist, or addiction counselor. It will be all too easy to spiral into self-loathing, completely defeating our recovery, if we work this step alone. We're going to need someone in our corner for this, we're going deep diving!

And just to be clear, a qualified sponsor is someone who has taken *ALL 12 STEPS* as laid out in the Big Book of *Alcoholics Anonymous*. Also, we need to be sure that the sponsor we chose to work with is present and leading us through and ready and available to answer all our questions. This is one of the biggest reasons we have sponsors. If there is anything that we are unsure of, we should not hesitate to ask our sponsor. Of course, we might want to prepare for some long talks!

Step One of Alcoholics Anonymous is the foundation upon which the entire 12-Step program is built. It represents a crucial turning point for alcoholics and other addicts as it marks the start of our journey towards sobriety and recovery, and a better life.

The purpose of Step One is to help us acknowledge and accept that we have a problem with alcohol or other addiction and that we are powerless to overcome it on our own. Through this step, we are encouraged to reach out for help and seek support from others, including the 12 Step community. By working through Step One, we are able to gain a new perspective on our lives and begin the process of reclaiming control over our thoughts, feelings, and actions. This step sets the stage for the growth and change that will occur throughout the rest of the 12 Step program.

Step One is a vital step in the recovery process because it involves acknowledging that our addiction has taken control of us and that we are no longer able to manage our life on our own. Admitting this can be a difficult and intimidating step, but it is necessary if we are going to move forward in our recovery. We simply cannot properly work any other step until we firmly have this one.

The purpose of this Step One workbook is to provide guidance and support as we take the first step towards recovery, and to help us begin the process of letting go of the grip that our addiction has on us and our life.

Using a Step One workbook will help us explore our own experiences with addiction and the ways in which it has affected our life. It can also help us recognize the benefits of admitting powerlessness and surrendering to our addiction and the recovery process. It provides a safe and supportive space for self-reflection and encourages us to seek the help and support we need as we work through the first of the 12 Steps of recovery. It is indeed an important first step towards a healthier and far more fulfilling future.

As diligently as we might work this first step, there will be things that we will forget or otherwise feel like we should have included but didn't. We have lived a thousand lives; it would be impossible to remember all of it at once. As long as we are honest and thorough in the working of step one to the best of our ability, as we move through the other steps, there will be time to revisit this one, and will actually become the norm.

While this book is a useful tool on your road to recovery, it does NOT replace the need for a sponsor or other addiction recovery specialist. While it is not necessarily needed, I strongly encourage you to incorporate group counseling for addicts as well as individual counseling with a professional that specializes in trauma and or addiction recovery, along with your meetings at a 12 step or secular group to fully round out your recovery program. You're likely to meet your demons along this road so you're gonna want someone in your corner.

Now then, let us first get a look at the layout of this workbook, shall we?

First, you will find six pages for notes right after this intro specifically for step 1. You will find call out boxes on every page for things that stand out. These pages are designed to help us keep our Step One notes organized.

The next section is a Trigger Tracker. While we might have made the decision to recover, that doesn't mean that we won't be triggered. In fact, for some of us, our triggers are far more frequent and intense in the beginning of our recovery. Tracking our triggers and reflecting on them can help us to identify some of our patterns and how we sabotage ourself in many areas of our life. Once we can see these, we can begin to make plans to shift them. Afterall, we can't change our patterns if we don't know what they are.

We might find that the trigger tracker will become a useful tool to use while we are working through Step One and beyond because it can help us to discover new things about ourselves that we will need for our road to recovery. Thoughtfully using the trigger tracker could also help us to diffuse some of our triggers.

NOTE: The trigger Tracker is *NOT* meant to replace calling your sponsor when you get triggered. You should *ALWAYS* contact your sponsor whenever you are struggling with an urge.

Next you will find supporting information on Step One and its importance.

In the largest section, you will find over 130 thought-provoking questions and exercises divided into six parts. All of the questions and exercises are specifically related to working Step One. Remember, there are no right or wrong answers, only your perceptions and reflections to get to know yourself and your addiction better so you can come into a place to be able accept yourself more fully. It would be wise to go over these with your sponsor.

Please don't rush to get this workbook done as quickly as possible, this is no race here. It's not like you're going to check the 12 steps off your to do list and be done with it. This is a life long journey. Take your time, answer thoughtfully, and be completely and brutally honest with yourself as if your life depends on it...because it does.

The last section is the self-dated daily journal to help support us while we are taking this first step. This is where we will spend a few minutes each morning on our plans for the day and each evening on our reflections from throughout the day. There are 42 days of full-page entries for our daily goals, plans, moods, gratitude's, and other recovery prompts specific to Step One. You'll also find check-off boxes for personal care and recovery check-ins. Every seven pages you will find a weekly check-in as well. Here you will reflect on the week just past and the one ahead.

As an afterthought, I added a couple of lists of coping strategies, activities, and self-care ideas as well as some contact pages where you can enter contacts for organizations, meeting members, and other contacts for your support network.

I have a clue where a road to recovery goes. And what that looks like. If I was able to survive it, so can you! Always remember to take good care of yourself. No one else will because no one else *can*. **It has to come from you**.

WE ADMITTED WE WERE POWERLESS OVER ALCOHOL – THAT OUR LIVES HAD BECOME UNMANAGEABLE

RECOMMENDED READINGS

DATE	WHAT I AM WORKING ON

MY FAVORITE STEP 1 QUOTE

STEP 1 PRINCIPLE

HONESTY

FIRST STEP PRAYER:

Help me to see and admit that I am powerless over my alcoholism. Help me to understand how my alcoholism has led to unmanageability in my life. Help me this day to understand the true meaning of powerlessness. Remove from me all denial of my alcoholism.

WHAT THIS MEANS TO ME:
first things first

HOW I HONORED
THE PRINCIPLE OF
Honesty

> But I've also learned I
> am not powerless over some
> things. I am not powerless
> over my attitudes. I am not
> powerless over negativity.
> I am not powerless over
> assuming responsibility
> for my own recovery."
>
> THE BIG BOOK

Trigger Tracker

Welcome to the trigger tracker! A trigger tracker is quite a useful in our recovery toolbox as it helps us to identify the specific situations, emotions, and circumstances that trigger our urge to drink or use. When we can recognize patterns in our triggers and urges, we can then learn to manage them in healthier ways.

By tracking the date, time, place, and specific trigger, we can gain a deeper understanding of our reactions and emotions. Furthermore, noting our knee-jerk reaction, physical sensations, thoughts, and feelings can help us identify patterns and develop strategies to either avoid or manage these triggers in the future. By reflecting on why a particular situation triggered us, we can gain deeper insight into our addiction and work towards healing and recovery. This information can help us to understand the root causes of our addiction, and to develop effective strategies to manage our cravings and avoid relapses.

By recording our triggers, we can become more aware of our behavior and thought patterns and make better-informed decisions to maintain our sobriety. Additionally, a trigger tracker can provide a visual representation of progress over time, and can help give us a sense of empowerment and increased hope for sustained, peaceful sobriety.

This Step 1 Workbook includes 103 guided trigger tracker entries for us to use while we are working through Step 1. For convenience purposes, I placed it in the front of the book so we have quick and easy access to it. Some of us will need to use this quite a bit!

Date: _____ Time: _____ Place: _____

What triggered me? _____

Knee-jerk reaction: _____

Physical sensation: _____

I thought: _____

I felt: _____

Why this triggered me

Date: _____ Time: _____ Place: _____

What triggered me? _____

Knee-jerk reaction: _____

Physical sensation: _____

I thought: _____

I felt: _____

Why this triggered me

Date: _____ Time: _____ Place: _____

What triggered me? _____

Knee-jerk reaction: _____

Physical sensation: _____

I thought: _____

I felt: _____

Why this triggered me

Date: _____ Time: _____ Place: _____

What triggered me? _____

Knee-jerk reaction: _____

Physical sensation: _____

I thought: _____

I felt: _____

Why this triggered me

Date: _____ Time: _____ Place: _____

What triggered me? _____

Knee-jerk reaction: _____

Physical sensation: _____

I thought: _____

I felt: _____

Why this triggered me

Date: _____ Time: _____ Place: _____

What triggered me? _____

Knee-jerk reaction: _____

Physical sensation: _____

I thought: _____

I felt: _____

Why this triggered me

Date: _____ Time: _____ Place: _____

What triggered me? _____

Knee-jerk reaction: _____

Physical sensation: _____

I thought: _____

I felt: _____

Why this triggered me

Date: _____ Time: _____ Place: _____

What triggered me? _____

Knee-jerk reaction: _____

Physical sensation: _____

I thought: _____

I felt: _____

Why this triggered me

Date: _____ Time: _____ Place: _____

What triggered me? _____

Knee-jerk reaction: _____

Physical sensation: _____

I thought: _____

I felt: _____

Why this triggered me

Date: _____ Time: _____ Place: _____

What triggered me? _____

Knee-jerk reaction: _____

Physical sensation: _____

I thought: _____

I felt: _____

Why this triggered me

Date: _____ Time: _____ Place: _____

What triggered me? _____

Knee-jerk reaction: _____

Physical sensation: _____

I thought: _____

I felt: _____

Why this triggered me

Date: _____ Time: _____ Place: _____

What triggered me? _____

Knee-jerk reaction: _____

Physical sensation: _____

I thought: _____

I felt: _____

Why this triggered me

Date: _____ Time: _____ Place: _____

What triggered me? _____

Knee-jerk reaction: _____

Physical sensation: _____

I thought: _____

I felt: _____

Why this triggered me

Date: _____ Time: _____ Place: _____

What triggered me? _____

Knee-jerk reaction: _____

Physical sensation: _____

I thought: _____

I felt: _____

Why this triggered me

Date: _____ Time: _____ Place: _____

What triggered me? _____

Knee-jerk reaction: _____

Physical sensation: _____

I thought: _____

I felt: _____

Why this triggered me

Date: _____ Time: _____ Place: _____

What triggered me? _____

Knee-jerk reaction: _____

Physical sensation: _____

I thought: _____

I felt: _____

Why this triggered me

Date: _____ Time: _____ Place: _____

What triggered me? _____

Knee-jerk reaction: _____

Physical sensation: _____

I thought: _____

I felt: _____

Why this triggered me

Date: _____ Time: _____ Place: _____

What triggered me? _____

Knee-jerk reaction: _____

Physical sensation: _____

I thought: _____

I felt: _____

Why this triggered me

Date: _____ Time: _____ Place: _____

What triggered me? _____

Knee-jerk reaction: _____

Physical sensation: _____

I thought: _____

I felt: _____

Why this triggered me

Date: _____ Time: _____ Place: _____

What triggered me? _____

Knee-jerk reaction: _____

Physical sensation: _____

I thought: _____

I felt: _____

Why this triggered me

Date: _____ Time: _____ Place: _____

What triggered me? _____

Knee-jerk reaction: _____

Physical sensation: _____

I thought: _____

I felt: _____

Why this triggered me

Date: _____ Time: _____ Place: _____

What triggered me? _____

Knee-jerk reaction: _____

Physical sensation: _____

I thought: _____

I felt: _____

Why this triggered me

Date: _____ Time: _____ Place: _____

What triggered me? _____

Knee-jerk reaction: _____

Physical sensation: _____

I thought: _____

I felt: _____

Why this triggered me

Date: _____ Time: _____ Place: _____

What triggered me? _____

Knee-jerk reaction: _____

Physical sensation: _____

I thought: _____

I felt: _____

Why this triggered me

Date: _____ Time: _____ Place: _____

What triggered me? _____

Knee-jerk reaction: _____

Physical sensation: _____

I thought: _____

I felt: _____

Why this triggered me

Date: _____ Time: _____ Place: _____

What triggered me? _____

Knee-jerk reaction: _____

Physical sensation: _____

I thought: _____

I felt: _____

Why this triggered me

Date: _____ Time: _____ Place: _____

What triggered me? _____

Knee-jerk reaction: _____

Physical sensation: _____

I thought: _____

I felt: _____

Why this triggered me

Date: _____ Time: _____ Place: _____

What triggered me? _____

Knee-jerk reaction: _____

Physical sensation: _____

I thought: _____

I felt: _____

Why this triggered me

Date: _____ Time: _____ Place: _____

What triggered me? _____

Knee-jerk reaction: _____

Physical sensation: _____

I thought: _____

I felt: _____

Why this triggered me

Date: _____ Time: _____ Place: _____

What triggered me? _____

Knee-jerk reaction: _____

Physical sensation: _____

I thought: _____

I felt: _____

Why this triggered me

Date: _____ Time: _____ Place: _____

What triggered me? _____

Knee-jerk reaction: _____

Physical sensation: _____

I thought: _____

I felt: _____

Why this triggered me

Date: _____ Time: _____ Place: _____

What triggered me? _____

Knee-jerk reaction: _____

Physical sensation: _____

I thought: _____

I felt: _____

Why this triggered me

Date: _____ Time: _____ Place: _____

What triggered me? _____

Knee-jerk reaction: _____

Physical sensation: _____

I thought: _____

I felt: _____

Why this triggered me

Date: _____ Time: _____ Place: _____

What triggered me? _____

Knee-jerk reaction: _____

Physical sensation: _____

I thought: _____

I felt: _____

Why this triggered me

Date: _____ Time: _____ Place: _____

What triggered me? _____

Knee-jerk reaction: _____

Physical sensation: _____

I thought: _____

I felt: _____

Why this triggered me

Date: _____ Time: _____ Place: _____

What triggered me? _____

Knee-jerk reaction: _____

Physical sensation: _____

I thought: _____

I felt: _____

Why this triggered me

Date: _____ Time: _____ Place: _____

What triggered me? _____

Knee-jerk reaction: _____

Physical sensation: _____

I thought: _____

I felt: _____

Why this triggered me

Date: _____ Time: _____ Place: _____

What triggered me? _____

Knee-jerk reaction: _____

Physical sensation: _____

I thought: _____

I felt: _____

Why this triggered me

Date: _____ Time: _____ Place: _____

What triggered me? _____

Knee-jerk reaction: _____

Physical sensation: _____

I thought: _____

I felt: _____

Why this triggered me

Date: _____ Time: _____ Place: _____

What triggered me? _____

Knee-jerk reaction: _____

Physical sensation: _____

I thought: _____

I felt: _____

Why this triggered me

Date: _____ Time: _____ Place: _____

What triggered me? _____

Knee-jerk reaction: _____

Physical sensation: _____

I thought: _____

I felt: _____

Why this triggered me

Date: _____ Time: _____ Place: _____

What triggered me? _____

Knee-jerk reaction: _____

Physical sensation: _____

I thought: _____

I felt: _____

Why this triggered me

Date: _____ Time: _____ Place: _____

What triggered me? _____

Knee-jerk reaction: _____

Physical sensation: _____

I thought: _____

I felt: _____

Why this triggered me

Date: _____ Time: _____ Place: _____

What triggered me? _____

Knee-jerk reaction: _____

Physical sensation: _____

I thought: _____

I felt: _____

Why this triggered me

Date: _____ Time: _____ Place: _____

What triggered me? _____

Knee-jerk reaction: _____

Physical sensation: _____

I thought: _____

I felt: _____

Why this triggered me

Date: _____ Time: _____ Place: _____

What triggered me? _____

Knee-jerk reaction: _____

Physical sensation: _____

I thought: _____

I felt: _____

Why this triggered me

Date: _____ Time: _____ Place: _____

What triggered me? _____

Knee-jerk reaction: _____

Physical sensation: _____

I thought: _____

I felt: _____

Why this triggered me

Date: _____ Time: _____ Place: _____

What triggered me? _____

Knee-jerk reaction: _____

Physical sensation: _____

I thought: _____

I felt: _____

Why this triggered me

Date: _____ Time: _____ Place: _____

What triggered me? _____

Knee-jerk reaction: _____

Physical sensation: _____

I thought: _____

I felt: _____

Why this triggered me

Date: _____ Time: _____ Place: _____

What triggered me? _____

Knee-jerk reaction: _____

Physical sensation: _____

I thought: _____

I felt: _____

Why this triggered me

Date: _____ Time: _____ Place: _____

What triggered me? _____

Knee-jerk reaction: _____

Physical sensation: _____

I thought: _____

I felt: _____

Why this triggered me

Date: _____ Time: _____ Place: _____

What triggered me? _____

Knee-jerk reaction: _____

Physical sensation: _____

I thought: _____

I felt: _____

Why this triggered me

Date: _____ Time: _____ Place: _____

What triggered me? _____

Knee-jerk reaction: _____

Physical sensation: _____

I thought: _____

I felt: _____

Why this triggered me

Date: _____ Time: _____ Place: _____

What triggered me? _____

Knee-jerk reaction: _____

Physical sensation: _____

I thought: _____

I felt: _____

Why this triggered me

Date: _____ Time: _____ Place: _____

What triggered me? _____

Knee-jerk reaction: _____

Physical sensation: _____

I thought: _____

I felt: _____

Why this triggered me

Date: _____ Time: _____ Place: _____

What triggered me? _____

Knee-jerk reaction: _____

Physical sensation: _____

I thought: _____

I felt: _____

Why this triggered me

Date: _____ Time: _____ Place: _____

What triggered me? _____

Knee-jerk reaction: _____

Physical sensation: _____

I thought: _____

I felt: _____

Why this triggered me

Date: _____ Time: _____ Place: _____

What triggered me? _____

Knee-jerk reaction: _____

Physical sensation: _____

I thought: _____

I felt: _____

Why this triggered me

Date: _____ Time: _____ Place: _____

What triggered me? _____

Knee-jerk reaction: _____

Physical sensation: _____

I thought: _____

I felt: _____

Why this triggered me

Date: _____ Time: _____ Place: _____

What triggered me? _____

Knee-jerk reaction: _____

Physical sensation: _____

I thought: _____

I felt: _____

Why this triggered me

Date: _____ Time: _____ Place: _____

What triggered me? _____

Knee-jerk reaction: _____

Physical sensation: _____

I thought: _____

I felt: _____

Why this triggered me

Date: _____ Time: _____ Place: _____

What triggered me? _____

Knee-jerk reaction: _____

Physical sensation: _____

I thought: _____

I felt: _____

Why this triggered me

Date: _____ Time: _____ Place: _____

What triggered me? _____

Knee-jerk reaction: _____

Physical sensation: _____

I thought: _____

I felt: _____

Why this triggered me

Date: _____ Time: _____ Place: _____

What triggered me? _____

Knee-jerk reaction: _____

Physical sensation: _____

I thought: _____

I felt: _____

Why this triggered me

Date: _____ Time: _____ Place: _____

What triggered me? _____

Knee-jerk reaction: _____

Physical sensation: _____

I thought: _____

I felt: _____

Why this triggered me

Date: _____ Time: _____ Place: _____

What triggered me? _____

Knee-jerk reaction: _____

Physical sensation: _____

I thought: _____

I felt: _____

Why this triggered me

Date: _____ Time: _____ Place: _____

What triggered me? _____

Knee-jerk reaction: _____

Physical sensation: _____

I thought: _____

I felt: _____

Why this triggered me

Date: _____ Time: _____ Place: _____

What triggered me? _____

Knee-jerk reaction: _____

Physical sensation: _____

I thought: _____

I felt: _____

Why this triggered me

Date: _____ Time: _____ Place: _____

What triggered me? _____

Knee-jerk reaction: _____

Physical sensation: _____

I thought: _____

I felt: _____

Why this triggered me

Date: _____ Time: _____ Place: _____

What triggered me? _____

Knee-jerk reaction: _____

Physical sensation: _____

I thought: _____

I felt: _____

Why this triggered me

Date: _____ Time: _____ Place: _____

What triggered me? _____

Knee-jerk reaction: _____

Physical sensation: _____

I thought: _____

I felt: _____

Why this triggered me

Date: _____ Time: _____ Place: _____

What triggered me? _____

Knee-jerk reaction: _____

Physical sensation: _____

I thought: _____

I felt: _____

Why this triggered me

Date: _____ Time: _____ Place: _____

What triggered me? _____

Knee-jerk reaction: _____

Physical sensation: _____

I thought: _____

I felt: _____

Why this triggered me

Date: _____ Time: _____ Place: _____

What triggered me? _____

Knee-jerk reaction: _____

Physical sensation: _____

I thought: _____

I felt: _____

Why this triggered me

Date: _____ Time: _____ Place: _____

What triggered me? _____

Knee-jerk reaction: _____

Physical sensation: _____

I thought: _____

I felt: _____

Why this triggered me

Date: _____ Time: _____ Place: _____

What triggered me? _____

Knee-jerk reaction: _____

Physical sensation: _____

I thought: _____

I felt: _____

Why this triggered me

Date: _____ Time: _____ Place: _____

What triggered me? _____

Knee-jerk reaction: _____

Physical sensation: _____

I thought: _____

I felt: _____

Why this triggered me

Date: _____ Time: _____ Place: _____

What triggered me? _____

Knee-jerk reaction: _____

Physical sensation: _____

I thought: _____

I felt: _____

Why this triggered me

Date: _____ Time: _____ Place: _____

What triggered me? _____

Knee-jerk reaction: _____

Physical sensation: _____

I thought: _____

I felt: _____

Why this triggered me

Date: _____ Time: _____ Place: _____

What triggered me? _____

Knee-jerk reaction: _____

Physical sensation: _____

I thought: _____

I felt: _____

Why this triggered me

Date: _____ Time: _____ Place: _____

What triggered me? _____

Knee-jerk reaction: _____

Physical sensation: _____

I thought: _____

I felt: _____

Why this triggered me

Date: _____ Time: _____ Place: _____

What triggered me? _____

Knee-jerk reaction: _____

Physical sensation: _____

I thought: _____

I felt: _____

Why this triggered me

Date: _____ Time: _____ Place: _____

What triggered me? _____

Knee-jerk reaction: _____

Physical sensation: _____

I thought: _____

I felt: _____

Why this triggered me

Date: _____ Time: _____ Place: _____

What triggered me? _____

Knee-jerk reaction: _____

Physical sensation: _____

I thought: _____

I felt: _____

Why this triggered me

Date: _____ Time: _____ Place: _____

What triggered me? _____

Knee-jerk reaction: _____

Physical sensation: _____

I thought: _____

I felt: _____

Why this triggered me

Date: _____ Time: _____ Place: _____

What triggered me? _____

Knee-jerk reaction: _____

Physical sensation: _____

I thought: _____

I felt: _____

Why this triggered me

Date: _____ Time: _____ Place: _____

What triggered me? _____

Knee-jerk reaction: _____

Physical sensation: _____

I thought: _____

I felt: _____

Why this triggered me

Date: _____ Time: _____ Place: _____

What triggered me? _____

Knee-jerk reaction: _____

Physical sensation: _____

I thought: _____

I felt: _____

Why this triggered me

Date: _____ Time: _____ Place: _____

What triggered me? _____

Knee-jerk reaction: _____

Physical sensation: _____

I thought: _____

I felt: _____

Why this triggered me

Date: _____ Time: _____ Place: _____

What triggered me? _____

Knee-jerk reaction: _____

Physical sensation: _____

I thought: _____

I felt: _____

Why this triggered me

Date: _____ Time: _____ Place: _____

What triggered me? _____

Knee-jerk reaction: _____

Physical sensation: _____

I thought: _____

I felt: _____

Why this triggered me

Date: _____ Time: _____ Place: _____

What triggered me? _____

Knee-jerk reaction: _____

Physical sensation: _____

I thought: _____

I felt: _____

Why this triggered me

Date: _____ Time: _____ Place: _____

What triggered me? _____

Knee-jerk reaction: _____

Physical sensation: _____

I thought: _____

I felt: _____

Why this triggered me

Date: _____ Time: _____ Place: _____

What triggered me? _____

Knee-jerk reaction: _____

Physical sensation: _____

I thought: _____

I felt: _____

Why this triggered me

Date: _____ Time: _____ Place: _____

What triggered me? _____

Knee-jerk reaction: _____

Physical sensation: _____

I thought: _____

I felt: _____

Why this triggered me

Date: _____ Time: _____ Place: _____

What triggered me? _____

Knee-jerk reaction: _____

Physical sensation: _____

I thought: _____

I felt: _____

Why this triggered me

Date: _____ Time: _____ Place: _____

What triggered me? _____

Knee-jerk reaction: _____

Physical sensation: _____

I thought: _____

I felt: _____

Why this triggered me

Date: _____ Time: _____ Place: _____

What triggered me? _____

Knee-jerk reaction: _____

Physical sensation: _____

I thought: _____

I felt: _____

Why this triggered me

Step 1: Admitting We Are Powerless

We admitted we were powerless over alcohol – that our lives had become unmanageable.

Alcoholism is a disease that affects millions of people around the world. It is a chronic and progressive condition that can take control of our life, leading to devastating consequences for both us and those around us. In order to overcome this and achieve lasting sobriety, it is crucial for us to take the first step in the process: admitting powerlessness.

Who wants to admit that something that cannot think, feel, or love us could possibly have ultimate power over us? For many of us, it seems, alcohol has the ability to completely destroy our lives yet, at the same time, we look to it for our salvation. No one understands.

We know that if we drink, we will lose. We will find trouble with the law, trouble at work, trouble at home, trouble with our health. We might lose our driver's license, our job, our friends, or our significant other whom we love so much. We know that if we drink, we will eventually lose the people and things that really matter most to us.

We know our loved ones believe that we don't value them and that we would rather be drunk than to spend time with them. We know this is not true, but still, we choose a drink. We are driven to it. It makes no sense to choose to do something when you know full well it will only result in extreme pain and fatal loss. But we do it nonetheless. Stupidity?

I suppose it can be argued that perhaps the alcoholic is just that, stupid. What other reasoning could there be? But the ironic thing is that most alcoholics I know are quite intelligent. So why do we stupidly choose such pain and losses just for a drunk?

It's not "drunk" that most alcoholics are looking for, we seek to quiet the nasty monster inside their head. I have taken to calling it the addiction monster. This is what drives an alcoholic, or any addict for that matter. We simply cannot get any peace in our head until we have a drink, a hit, or whatever it is that we are addicted to. To this, we are powerless.

We struggle so hard to not drink so we can spend quality time with those we love. We desperately want this! We may, on occasion, win the argument we have in our head...for a minute. But then the monster gets all the bigger and louder and might even become belligerent. It is this we are powerless over. This is the reason my life became unmanageable. What's your story?

We don't realize that we have zero power over our addiction and that our lives have become unmanageable even through all the craziness. We just refuse to see this shit as crazy. We think we can control our drinking or addiction. We can go without it, we can cutback or stop, we are in control. When we get that first urge, we are able to restrain, maybe even without trouble. But then it comes back again, usually rather quickly and stronger. And we restrain again. Then it's back, more powerfully than before. Eventually, it gets to the point where it totally consumes our entire mind. We struggle so hard to refrain, to distract ourselves, to find something else to focus on. All to no avail!

Finally, after painfully struggling for some time, we cave. We drink or use, we have to if just for the mental relief so we can clear that out of our heads and get on with things. And yet, for so many years, we just don't see this as having absolutely no power over our addiction. Nor do we see this as being unmanageable. How funny we addicts are!

It took me decades to finally reach Step One. I don't mean working it, I mean just getting to the place where I finally realized that I had no control whatsoever, that I was powerless. This was quite a humbling experience for me. Most of us alcoholics and addicts are control freaks after all, including me!

Coming into that place also gave me the hope that I just might be able to finally quit for good. What an inspiring relief! I also realized that I needed help, that I couldn't do it alone or on my own terms. What a comforting feeling! It was then that I actually had a sense of safety. That I wasn't alone and with the help of others that have been there, I could become safe from my addiction. And that this safety could actually come from me. I could finally count on myself to take right care of me for the first time in decades. It was okay for me to love me! I was a valuable human too!

It can be difficult to come to terms with the reality that we are powerless over alcohol, but accepting that we are dependent on alcohol can give us back power over our life by helping us to focus on our recovery instead of dwelling on negative emotions.

This can give us strength by helping us to come to terms with the reality of our situation. It can provide us with a sense of relief and acceptance which can help us to take the necessary steps toward our recovery. Additionally, accepting our powerlessness can help to reduce feelings of shame, guilt, and embarrassment as it allows us to focus on the positive aspects of recovery instead of dwelling on negative feelings. Finally, accepting our powerlessness can provide us with the motivation and courage to seek help and take steps towards a healthier lifestyle.

I'm not the only one who found relief and a little peace from finally admitting that I was powerless and that my life had become unmanageable. Here are some quotes from others who found some solace in coming to this first step:

1. The first step was the hardest for me because I had to admit that I was powerless over my addiction and that it was controlling my life." - Anonymous
2. "Admitting powerlessness was like finally taking a deep breath after holding it for so long. I realized that **I didn't have to struggle anymore**, and that **I could finally let go and let someone help me**." - Lindsey B.
3. "I remember sitting in that first AA meeting and hearing the words *'We are powerless over alcohol and our lives have become unmanageable'* and it was like a lightbulb went off in my head. I realized that **I was not alone** and that **there was a solution**." - Joe M.
4. "**Step one was the turning point for me**. It was the moment when I finally faced the truth about my addiction and realized that I needed help." - John D.
5. "I had to surrender to the fact that I was powerless over my addiction **before I could start the journey of recovery. It was a difficult, but necessary step**." - Maria P.
6. "Admitting powerlessness was a humbling experience, but it was also **a moment of liberation**. I finally realized that **I didn't have to do this alone**, and that I could rely on the support and guidance of others." – Anonymous
7. "**Step one was a critical moment** in my recovery journey because it allowed me to finally **let go of the shame and guilt** I felt about my addiction. It **gave me the courage** to ask for help and start taking control of my life." - Sarah S.
8. "I was resistant to admitting my powerlessness over alcohol for a long time, but when I finally did, **it was like a weight lifted off my shoulders**. I realized that **I wasn't alone, and that there was hope for me**." - Mike R.
9. "The first step in recovery is admitting that we have a problem. This is **not a weakness, but a strength**. **It takes a lot of courage** and humility **to acknowledge our powerlessness**, but it is the first step towards a new life." - Mark T.
10. "**Admitting powerlessness was a pivotal moment for me** because it allowed me to start looking at my addiction objectively. It gave me the foundation I needed to build a new life in recovery." - Anonymous

These quotes highlight the challenges and benefits of admitting powerlessness over addiction and the role it plays in the recovery journey as well as the importance of taking the first step in the recovery process. Through 12-step and secular programs, support and guidance from others can be instrumental in helping us find the strength to overcome our addiction and move forward in recovery. By taking the first step and acknowledging our powerlessness, we can find the courage and support we need to begin the process of healing ourselves and moving forward in our recovery.

Personal stories of admitting powerlessness can be a powerful tool in inspiring us to continue to take this important step. The Big Book is full of stories of people who have found hope and recovery by admitting that they were powerless over alcohol. By sharing their experiences, these folks provide a shining example of the importance of humility and the benefits that come from admitting powerlessness. They provide encouragement and support for those of us who are just starting our journey. They also offer proof that Step One, and the hope that comes out of it, is a critical component of recovery and true sobriety. These stories serve as a reminder that recovery is indeed possible, and that hope can be found *through* the admission of powerlessness.

The step before Step One: Getting Clear About Our Journey

First, let's look at the reasons we drank or used. We might not remember all our reasons at once so we'll add to our list as we remember more. Once we have a number of reasons written down, we reflect on how we feel as we read over our list. Now we'll place an X next to the ones that we wish were not on our list.

Now, let's make a list of reasons we want change. We'll reflect on why we are seeking sobriety in the first place and add to the list as we discover more reasons. Let's spend a few minutes in quiet thought imagining how we might feel if we were to succeeded here.

Are there any reasons for sobriety that we wished were on our change list but aren't? We'll list them here and why we wished they were on our list. Why are they not on it?

Let's look at what scares us about continuing to drink or use:

What scares us about not drinking or using:

What sobriety actually mean to us:

What scares us the most about sobriety?

Let's spend a little time on what our main goal from sobriety is:

What are our long-term goals for sobriety and addiction recovery?

We have all lost things, many things, as well as missed out on opportunities due to our drinking or using. So, we honestly ask ourself, *"What do I want to get or get back through my sobriety?"*

What other things are we looking forward to as we work on our sobriety and recovery?

Self-care is important yet we alcoholics tend to overlook this. We have a tendency to neglect ourselves. Why is self-care more important for those of us on a journey to sobriety and recovery?

We need to take an honest look at our current self-care routine:

Admitting We Are Powerless

Honesty is the guiding principle of Step 1 in Alcoholics Anonymous. The first step involves admitting powerlessness over alcohol and acknowledging the reality of our addiction. Honesty is critical in this process because it requires us to be truthful with ourselves about the extent of our addiction. By admitting the truth about our addiction, we can begin to break free from denial and take responsibility for our actions. Honesty allows us to *understand the depth of our addiction* and begin our journey towards recovery. It also lays the foundation for trust and openness, which are crucial elements in the recovery process. By embracing honesty, we can build a strong foundation for our recovery and set the stage for a life free from the grip of alcohol.

Admitting powerlessness is a crucial component of the recovery process for those of us struggling with alcohol and addiction. It involves acknowledging that the alcohol or addiction has taken over our life and that we are unable to control our alcohol or substance consumption. This realization can be difficult to come to, as it requires us to be brutally honest and completely vulnerable about our situation. However, it is an essential step in the journey towards recovery.

One of the main reasons that admitting powerlessness is so important is because it allows us to relinquish control of our addiction and seek the help we need. When we acknowledge that we are unable to control our alcohol consumption, we can take the first step towards seeking support and guidance from others who have been through the same experience. This support can come in many forms, including 12-step programs like Alcoholics Anonymous®, therapy, or rehabilitation.

Admitting powerlessness also helps us to break free from the cycle of denial that often accompanies addiction. Denial is a defense mechanism that allows us to ignore the reality of our situation and to justify our behavior, no matter how hurtful it might be. By acknowledging that we are powerless over our addiction, we can finally come out of of denial and begin to see the need for change.

Another reason why admitting powerlessness is important is because it allows us to take responsibility for our actions. By acknowledging that our alcoholism or addiction has taken over our life and that we are unable to control it, we can take responsibility for the impact that our addiction has had on both ourselves and those around us. This sense of responsibility can help to motivate us to take the necessary steps towards lasting, peaceful sobriety.

Finally, admitting powerlessness can help us to understand the nature of addiction and to see that it is a disease that affects not only us but also our loved ones and others around us. This recognition can help us to see the need for change and to take the first step towards recovery.

Admitting powerlessness is a humbling experience, but it is an essential step in the recovery process. It requires us to set aside our ego and acknowledge that we have been unable to control our alcohol or substance consumption, and that it has taken over our lives. Humility is a key aspect of this step, as it allows us to be more open to seeking help and to take the first step towards recovery.

The Big Book of Alcoholics Anonymous encourages us to embrace humility in our journey towards recovery and sobriety. It states, "*We are not a worthy bunch. We are compulsive people who have been addicted to a fatal substance and left to our own devices, we would drink it to our death.*" By acknowledging the reality of our situation, we can recognize our need for help and begin to believe that recovery is possible, even for us.

Admitting powerlessness can be a difficult and humbling experience, but it also brings with it many benefits. By acknowledging our inability to control our alcohol or substance consumption, we can begin to see a path to a better future. The benefits of admitting powerlessness are numerous, and they are essential components of recovery.

One of the main benefits of admitting powerlessness is that it can bring a sense of relief. For many of us, alcoholism and addiction can be a source of immense shame and guilt. Admitting powerlessness allows us to release these negative feelings and move forward with our recovery. The Big Book of Alcoholics Anonymous states, "*We will not regret the past nor wish to shut the door on it.*" By admitting powerlessness, we can begin to let go of the past and focus on the future.

Another benefit of admitting powerlessness is that it can lead to greater self-awareness. By acknowledging our inability to control our alcohol or substance consumption, we can begin to understand our motivations and triggers. This self-awareness can be an essential tool in the recovery process, as we can use it to better understand ourselves and our addiction. The Big Book of Alcoholics Anonymous states, "*We will comprehend the word serenity and we will know peace.*"

Admitting powerlessness can also lead to greater accountability. By acknowledging our alcoholism or addiction, we can take responsibility for our actions and begin to make positive changes in our lives. The Big Book of Alcoholics Anonymous states, "*We will get down to causes and conditions. We will not blame others nor blame ourselves. We will take what we have learned and use it for growth.*" By admitting powerlessness, we can begin to take control of our lives and work towards recovery.

Reduced stress and anxiety, increased self-awareness, and improved relationships with loved ones are a few more of the benefits that we can expect. The Big Book of Alcoholics Anonymous states, "*We have come to believe that a power greater than ourselves can restore us to sanity.*" By embracing humility and admitting powerlessness, we can begin to access the support we need to overcome our addiction.

We also open the door to greater hope when we admit that we are powerless. By acknowledging our addiction and our inability to control our consumption, we can begin to see a path to a better future. Hope is an essential component of recovery, and it is often born from admitting powerlessness. Hope can provide us with the strength and encouragement we need to continue on our journey. By admitting powerlessness, we can begin to believe that recovery is possible and that a better life awaits us. This newfound hope can be a source of strength and encouragement in our journey towards sobriety.

Hope is not just a positive feeling; it is a critical component of recovery. Research has shown that individuals with hope have a better chance of overcoming their addiction, as they are more likely to seek help and engage in treatment. The Big Book of Alcoholics Anonymous recognizes this, stating, "*We have seen the truth demonstrated again and again: that those who have honestly faced their problems in surrender to a higher power are lifted from the muck of a helpless state to a plane of usefulness, happiness, and peace.*"

When did you first suspect that you might be an alcoholic or addict?

What lies have you told ourself to excuse your alcoholism or addiction?

What lies have you told others to excuse your alcoholism or addiction?

When did you first toy with the idea that you were powerless over alcohol or addiction?

When was the first time you, however briefly, admitted to yourself that you have a problem with drinking or addiction?

How did you feel about that?

When was the first time you, however briefly, admitted to someone else that you have a problem with drinking or addiction?

How did you feel about that?

How long was it before you admitted it again?

How many times have you tried to quit drinking or using?

What led you to admitting you have a drinking problem or attempting to quit in the past?

How do you feel when you think about admitting that you are powerlessness over alcohol or your addiction and that your life has become unmanageable?

What would be so bad in admitting that you are completely powerless over alcohol or your addiction?

Write a letter to yourself from the perspective of your alcoholism or addiction. Describe the ways in which it has taken control of your life and the negative consequences it has caused.

What are the benefits of admitting that you are powerless over alcohol or your addiction and that your life has become unmanageable?

How do you think your life could be different if you were to admit that you were powerless over alcohol or your addiction?

What fears or concerns do you have about admitting you're powerless over alcohol or addiction?

How has the idea of powerlessness impacted your previous attempts to quit?

How do you think accepting your powerlessness can help you in your journey to recovery?

How does accepting your powerlessness change your perspective on alcohol or your addiction?

What were some events or circumstances that led you to acknowledge your powerlessness?

Have you ever sought help like AA, NA, or addiction counseling, prior to now, to overcome your alcoholism or addiction?

Our Unmanageable Life

The concept of a life becoming unmanageable is a critical component of the first step of all 12-step programs. This first step requires us to acknowledge and admit that we are powerless over alcohol and that our lives have become unmanageable as a result.

This concept of an unmanageable life is a pivotal moment for us in the journey towards sobriety. The acknowledgement of powerlessness over alcohol and the realization that our life has become unmanageable are crucial for initiating the process of recovery and healing.

A life becoming unmanageable is a term used to describe the negative effects that alcoholism and addiction can have on one's life. An unmanageable life is characterized by various negative consequences which are caused by excessive alcohol consumption. These effects can be seen in a variety of ways including financial problems, relationship difficulties, physical health issues, emotional distress, and even legal problems. For example, we may find that we are spending more money on alcohol than we can actually afford or getting a DUI, leading to financial and potentially legal difficulties. We may also experience strained relationships with friends, family, and coworkers as a result of our drinking.

Physical health problems are also a common effect of alcoholism and addiction, including liver damage, high blood pressure, and various forms of cancer. These health problems can result in chronic pain and discomfort, further exacerbating the stress and anxiety associated with addiction. Additionally, emotional distress such as depression and anxiety are often experienced by alcoholics and addicts.

The constant cycle of drinking or using, followed by negative consequences, and more drinking, creates a vicious cycle that is difficult to break. In fact, the negative garbage that comes up for us will have us drinking or using all the more. This cycle can leave us feeling hopeless and helpless, unable to control our drinking and the impact it has on our lives.

The first step is designed to help us understand and acknowledge the negative impact that our addiction is having on our lives. By admitting that our lives have become unmanageable, we are able to begin to work towards regaining control over our lives. This admission is a critical component of recovery, as it allows us to face our addiction and begin the process of healing and recovery. This then allows us to begin to address the physical, emotional, and psychological effects of addiction, ultimately leading to a better and more fulfilling life.

In what ways has your alcoholism or addiction become unmanageable?

How has alcohol or addiction kept you from living your best life?

How much time and money have you spent drinking or using?

How does alcoholism or addiction get in the way of your dreams?

How has your addiction impacted your relationships with others?

How do you envision your relationships changing as you work towards sobriety and recovery?

What are some negative consequences you've suffered as a result of your alcoholism or addiction?

Recall some examples of the ways your alcoholism or addiction caused harm to yourself?

And to others?

How has your alcoholism or addiction affected your physical well-being?

Your emotional well-being?

Your social well-being?

What are some of the triggers or stressors that cause you to drink or use drugs?

How can you identify and address your triggers in a healthy way?

What are some of the things you can do to reduce stress and maintain a balanced lifestyle?

What are some coping mechanisms you can use to handle negative emotions or cravings?

How can you build a support team to help you stay accountable and on track with your goals?

How can you create a routine or structure that helps you maintain your sobriety and improve your mental and physical well-being?

How can you avoid self-harm or neglect?

How can you make positive changes that align with your values and support your recovery?

What are some strategies you can use to avoid or limit your exposure to people, places, or things that may trigger you to drink or use?

What steps can you take to reduce the financial stress related to your addiction or alcoholism?

What steps can you take to reduce relationship stress related to your addiction or alcoholism?

How can you deal with boredom or other challenges that may arise during your recovery?

What it is to Surrender

Surrender is a crucial part of recovery through 12-step programs. In AA's first step, we must admit that we are powerless over alcohol and that our lives have become unmanageable.

Surrender is the act of letting go of control and recognizing the need for help in overcoming addiction. This can be a difficult and emotional process, but it is essential for us to understand and embrace the concept of surrender in order to move forward in our recovery journey.

For many us, control is a central issue. We may feel like we have lost control over our lives and our substance use, but at the same time, we still hold on to the belief that we can manage it on our own. This can create a vicious cycle of repeated failures, leading to feelings of hopelessness and despair. It is only through surrendering to the reality of our addiction and acknowledging our powerlessness over it that we can begin to heal and move forward.

Surrendering to the power of addiction is not a sign of weakness. Rather, it is an act of strength, as we must overcome our fear and ego in order to ask for help. By admitting that we cannot solve the problem on our own, we open the door to a new perspective and a new way of life. It is a crucial step towards accepting responsibility for our actions and beginning the healing process.

For many of us, surrendering to addiction and admitting powerlessness can be a difficult and emotional process. We may feel like we are giving up control, which can be scary and unfamiliar. We may also have internalized negative beliefs about addiction and shame surrounding our substance use, which can make it even harder to surrender.

However, it is important for us to understand that surrendering to addiction is not the same as giving up on ourselves. Instead, it is a necessary step towards regaining control and taking our lives back. Surrendering allows us to acknowledge our addiction, seek help, and begin the journey towards recovery.

Overcoming resistance to surrender can be challenging, but with support, guidance, and self-care, we can begin to let go of control and embrace a new way of life. By working the first step, we can gain the support, guidance, and tools we need to achieve and maintain lasting sobriety.

What is it about sobriety that scares you?

What is it about sobriety that excites you?

What does surrendering to your alcoholism or addiction and the recovery process mean to you?

How do you feel when you think about surrendering to your alcoholism or addiction?

What are some of the things you're afraid of surrendering or letting go of as you work on sobriety?

When have you surrendered in the past, and how did it impact the outcome?

What would happen if you tried to quit drinking or using without surrendering?

How do you think surrendering to your addiction or alcoholism can help you in your recovery?

What are the benefits of surrendering to your alcoholism or addiction and the recovery process?

What would surrendering to addiction or alcoholism require of you?

How does surrendering to addiction or alcoholism help you find peace and serenity?

What are the risks of not surrendering to addiction or alcoholism?

What would surrendering to addiction or alcoholism mean for your future?

For your relationships with others?

_____
_____
_____
_____
_____
_____
_____

For your physical and emotional well-being?

_____
_____
_____
_____
_____
_____
_____
_____

What are some of the challenges you anticipate in surrendering to addiction or alcoholism?

_____
_____
_____
_____
_____
_____
_____

What are the steps you need to take to surrender to addiction or alcoholism?

To Error is human. Embrace your humanness. Practice writing and saying, 10 or more times, your name and your addiction. Sometimes it takes practice admitting something before we can get it through our heads. Example: I'm Diana and I'm an alcoholic.

Write a letter to yourself explaining that you are an alcoholic or addict.

Write a letter of apology to yourself for not wanting to get sober.

Write a letter of apology to yourself for wanting to get sober.

Now write a letter responding to your previous letters, understanding and forgiving yourself for your alcoholism or addiction, for not wanting sobriety, and for wanting sobriety.

Practice self-compassion and self-care:

Self-compassion and self-care are essential components for addiction recovery. The first step is admitting powerlessness over alcohol and recognizing that our life has become unmanageable. However, this process can be incredibly challenging and overwhelming for us. That's why it is essential for us to practice self-compassion and self-care in order to support our journey towards sobriety.

Self-compassion involves treating ourself with kindness, understanding, and empathy, even in the face of difficult experiences. It is recognizing that our struggles are a normal part of the human experience, and that everyone makes mistakes and faces challenges in life. By being gentle with ourself and avoiding self-criticism, we can reduce feelings of shame and guilt, which are often triggers for substance abuse.

Self-care is the practice of taking care of one's physical, emotional, and mental well-being. This can include activities such as exercise, mindfulness, healthy eating, and getting adequate sleep. By engaging in self-care activities, we can reduce stress and promote relaxation, which can make it easier to resist cravings and avoid relapse. Additionally, self-care can help us develop a positive relationship with our bodies and minds, which can boost self-esteem and confidence, further supporting our journey towards recovery.

One of the key challenges in overcoming addiction is the belief that alcohol or drugs will provide the comfort, relief, or happiness that we seek. By practicing self-compassion and self-care, we can learn to find comfort and happiness in other, healthier ways. We can learn to rely on ourselves for support and to take care of our own needs, rather than turning to substances for relief. This is a critical step towards overcoming addiction and achieving a fulfilling and sober life.

What does self-compassion mean to you?

What is the difference between self-compassion and self-pity?

What are some of the benefits of self-compassion and self-care?

What are some of the negative thoughts or beliefs that you have about yourself or your alcoholism or addiction?

How can you challenge and reframe these thoughts as you move toward sobriety?

How do you typically speak to yourself when you make a mistake or face a challenge?

_____
_____
_____
_____
_____
_____
_____

What are some things that you might say to a good friend who is struggling with a similar issue?

_____
_____
_____
_____
_____
_____
_____

How can you apply the same gentile kindness and understanding to yourself?

_____
_____
_____
_____
_____
_____

What else can you do to be kind and gentle with yourself as you work on your sobriety?

How does practicing self-compassion and self-care help you in your journey towards sobriety?

What are some obstacles that might prevent you from practicing self-compassion and self-care?

What do you need to work on to become kinder and more compassionate to yourself?

What are some of the things you need to do to take care of yourself?

How can you support yourself and prioritize practicing self-care as you work towards sobriety?

What self-care activities you've done in the past that made you feel good about yourself?

What are some self-care activities or practices that you enjoy or find helpful?

How can you incorporate these into your routine?

How can you be more understanding and patient with yourself as you work towards recovery?

How can you remind yourself that recovery is a journey and it's normal to have ups and downs?

What are some ways you can maintain self-compassion and understanding when faced with setbacks in your recovery journey?

What are some things that you can do to practice self-compassion when you are feeling overwhelmed or discouraged?

How else can you practice self-compassion as you work towards the recovery process?

How can you balance self-compassion and self-care with accountability and taking responsibility for your actions?

What are some things you can do to support yourself in moments of temptation or triggers?

What self-care activities can help you manage stress and anxiety as you work on your sobriety?

What are some positive affirmations or mantras that you can use to help you practice self-compassion and self-care?

How can you continue to build and strengthen your self-compassion and self-care skills as you progress in your recovery journey?

Self-reflection:

Self-reflection is also an important aspect of addiction recovery. It is a process of examining our thoughts, behaviors, and emotions in a non-judgmental way to gain a deeper understanding of ourself and our relationship with alcohol. Self-reflection can help us see the impact that alcohol has had on our life and recognize the need for change.

Through self-reflection, we can identify patterns of behavior and thought that have contributed to our addiction. We can explore the reasons behind our drinking and recognize the root causes of our problem. This can include examining past traumas, family history, and personal beliefs and values.

Self-reflection can also help us see the harm that our drinking has caused to ourselves and those around us. It can lead to feelings of guilt, shame, and regret, but it is important to remember that these feelings are a normal part of the recovery process. By accepting responsibility for our actions, we can begin to work on making amends and building a new, healthier life which includes healthier relationships.

In addition to the benefits mentioned above, self-reflection can also help us gain insight into our motivations and goals. By examining our values and aspirations, we can make a plan for our future that aligns with our highest priorities. This can help us stay focused on our sobriety and avoid falling back into old patterns.

By engaging in self-reflection, individuals can gain insight, acceptance, and a sense of purpose in their journey towards sobriety.

What are some challenges or difficulties you faced recently, and how have you coped with them?

How do you typically react to stress or challenges, and how can you work on managing your emotions in a healthy way?

What are some things that you are proud of or that have gone well recently?

What are some areas of your life that you would like to work on improving or focusing on?

What are some things that you are grateful for in your life?

What are some things that you value or prioritize in your life?

What are some of the things you're most proud of about yourself?

What are some of the things you love about yourself?

What are some of the things you need to forgive yourself for?

What are some things that trigger your cravings, and how can you manage them?

How have your personal values and beliefs been impacted by your addiction?

How can you work towards aligning your actions with your values and beliefs?

Write a letter to yourself admitting your powerlessness over addiction and that you are now seeking/getting help for sustainable sobriety.

What are some ways you can celebrate your progress and recognize your efforts in the recovery journey, even when it feels small?

How can you stay motivated and focused on your sobriety, even when you feel like giving up?

How has your understanding of your addiction or alcoholism changed since beginning recovery?

What have you learned about yourself so far in your recovery process?

What are some ways you can prioritize self-reflection and introspection in your recovery?

What are some techniques or exercises that you find helpful for self-reflection and introspection?

How can you challenge any negative thoughts and beliefs that you have about yourself, and reframe them positively?

What are some things you can do to maintain a positive and healthy mindset as you work towards sobriety?

In what ways can you cultivate a growth mindset, and continue to evolve in your sobriety?

How do you see your future, sober self?

What steps will you take to ensure you continue making progress towards your sobriety goals?

What are some things that bring you joy or fulfillment, and how can you make time for them?

The daily Journal

The daily journal covers a wide range of topics specifically related to Step 1 and is a great tool for those of us who continue to work on this step.

The daily AA cliché helps us to stay focused on the recovery process.

The mood rating, daily goals, and plans for the day help to provide structure and direction.

The daily reflection on positive things done, realizations and clarities, gratitude, interactions with others, and thoughts and feelings related to alcohol or addiction help to provide a comprehensive understanding of our emotional and mental state.

The self-care check-ins help ensure that we are taking care of our physical and emotional well-being, which is essential in the recovery process.

The reflection on the powerlessness over alcohol, what we are learning to accept or surrender, and our struggles can help us gain insight into our addiction and what we need to work on to achieve lasting sobriety.

The entry on our progress so far helps us see our progress and stay motivated in our recovery journey.

By reflecting on what we did to make our life more manageable, we can see the practical steps we are taking towards recovery and better understand the connection between our actions and our progress in recovery. It can also help us identify areas where we can make improvements and create new habits that support our recovery.

Coping strategies I'll use this coming week:

Last week's biggest struggle:

How I'll overcome it this week:

Last week's biggest win:

How I'll keep it up moving forward:

THIS WEEK'S TOP GOALS

1.
2.
3.

HOW I'LL ACCOMPLISH THEM

TOOLS & HELP I'LL USE

Date: _____ / _____ / _____   TODAY'S MOOD RATING: 1 2 3 4 5

DAILY CLICHÉ: *One day at a time*

Who I said something nice to and what I said:

_____
_____
_____

Thoughts or feelings I had related to alcohol today:

How I feel today about being powerless over alcohol:

_____
_____
_____
_____

I'm learning to accept or surrender:

A struggle I had and how I could have handled it better:

_____
_____
_____
_____
_____

What I did today to help make my life more manageable:

How I feel about my progress in recovery thus far:

TODAY'S ACTION LIST

Morning Prayer/Meditation ☑
Read Scripture/Recovery Lit ☑
Attended a Meeting ☑
Called Sponsor/Someone Sober ☑
Showered ☑   Teeth Brushed ☑
Water I Drank   1 2 3 4 5 6 7 8
Hours I Slept   1 2 3 4 5 6 7 8

TODAY'S GOALS

1. _____ ☑
2. _____ ☑
3. _____ ☑

TODAY'S PLANS	TIME

POSITIVE THINGS I DID TODAY

A REALIZATION OR CLARITY I HAD

TODAY I'M GRATEFUL FOR

Date: _____ / _____ / _____   TODAY'S MOOD RATING: 1 2 3 4 5

DAILY CLICHÉ: *Surrender to win*

Who I said something nice to and what I said:

Thoughts or feelings I had related to alcohol today:

How I feel today about being powerless over alcohol:

I'm learning to accept or surrender:

A struggle I had and how I could have handled it better:

What I did today to help make my life more manageable:

How I feel about my progress in recovery thus far:

TODAY'S ACTION LIST

Morning Prayer/Meditation ☐
Read Scripture/Recovery Lit ☐
Attended a Meeting ☐
Called Sponsor/Someone Sober ☐
Showered ☐   Teeth Brushed ☐
Water I Drank   1 2 3 4 5 6 7 8
Hours I Slept   1 2 3 4 5 6 7 8

TODAY'S GOALS

1. _____ ☐
2. _____ ☐
3. _____ ☐

TODAY'S PLANS	TIME

POSITIVE THINGS I DID TODAY

A REALIZATION OR CLARITY I HAD

TODAY I'M GRATEFUL FOR

91

Date: _____ / _____ / _____   TODAY'S MOOD RATING: 1 2 3 4 5

DAILY CLICHÉ: *Meeting makers make it*

Who I said something nice to and what I said:

_____
_____
_____

Thoughts or feelings I had related to alcohol today:

How I feel today about being powerless over alcohol:

_____
_____
_____

I'm learning to accept or surrender:

A struggle I had and how I could have handled it better:

_____
_____
_____
_____
_____

What I did today to help make my life more manageable:

How I feel about my progress in recovery thus far:

TODAY'S ACTION LIST

Morning Prayer/Meditation ☑
Read Scripture/Recovery Lit ☑
Attended a Meeting ☑
Called Sponsor/Someone Sober ☑
Showered ☑   Teeth Brushed ☑
Water I Drank   1 2 3 4 5 6 7 8
Hours I Slept   1 2 3 4 5 6 7 8

TODAY'S GOALS

1. _____ ☐
2. _____ ☐
3. _____ ☐

TODAY'S PLANS	TIME

POSITIVE THINGS I DID TODAY

A REALIZATION OR CLARITY I HAD

TODAY I'M GRATEFUL FOR

Date: _____ / _____ / _____   TODAY'S MOOD RATING: 1 2 3 4 5

DAILY CLICHÉ: *It works if you work it*

Who I said something nice to and what I said:

Thoughts or feelings I had related to alcohol today:

How I feel today about being powerless over alcohol:

I'm learning to accept or surrender:

A struggle I had and how I could have handled it better:

What I did today to help make my life more manageable:

How I feel about my progress in recovery thus far:

TODAY'S ACTION LIST

Morning Prayer/Meditation ☐
Read Scripture/Recovery Lit ☐
Attended a Meeting ☐
Called Sponsor/Someone Sober ☐
Showered ☐   Teeth Brushed ☐
Water I Drank   1 2 3 4 5 6 7 8
Hours I Slept   1 2 3 4 5 6 7 8

TODAY'S GOALS

1. _____ ☐
2. _____ ☐
3. _____ ☐

TODAY'S PLANS	TIME

POSITIVE THINGS I DID TODAY

A REALIZATION OR CLARITY I HAD

TODAY I'M GRATEFUL FOR

Date: _____ / _____ / _____   TODAY'S MOOD RATING: 1 2 3 4 5

DAILY CLICHÉ: *Easy does it*

Who I said something nice to and what I said:

_____

_____

_____

Thoughts or feelings I had related to alcohol today:

How I feel today about being powerless over alcohol:

_____

_____

_____

I'm learning to accept or surrender:

A struggle I had and how I could have handled it better:

_____

_____

_____

_____

_____

What I did today to help make my life more manageable:

How I feel about my progress in recovery thus far:

TODAY'S ACTION LIST

Morning Prayer/Meditation ☑

Read Scripture/Recovery Lit ☑

Attended a Meeting ☑

Called Sponsor/Someone Sober ☑

Showered ☑   Teeth Brushed ☑

Water I Drank   1 2 3 4 5 6 7 8

Hours I Slept   1 2 3 4 5 6 7 8

TODAY'S GOALS

1. _____ ☑

2. _____ ☑

3. _____ ☑

TODAY'S PLANS	TIME

POSITIVE THINGS I DID TODAY

A REALIZATION OR CLARITY I HAD

TODAY I'M GRATEFUL FOR

Date: _____ / _____ / _____   TODAY'S MOOD RATING: 1 2 3 4 5

DAILY CLICHÉ: *First things first*

Who I said something nice to and what I said:

Thoughts or feelings I had related to alcohol today:

How I feel today about being powerless over alcohol:

I'm learning to accept or surrender:

A struggle I had and how I could have handled it better:

What I did today to help make my life more manageable:

How I feel about my progress in recovery thus far:

TODAY'S ACTION LIST
Morning Prayer/Meditation ☐
Read Scripture/Recovery Lit ☐
Attended a Meeting ☐
Called Sponsor/Someone Sober ☐
Showered ☐   Teeth Brushed ☐
Water I Drank   1 2 3 4 5 6 7 8
Hours I Slept   1 2 3 4 5 6 7 8

TODAY'S GOALS
1. _____ ☐
2. _____ ☐
3. _____ ☐

TODAY'S PLANS	TIME

POSITIVE THINGS I DID TODAY

A REALIZATION OR CLARITY I HAD

TODAY I'M GRATEFUL FOR

Date: _____ / _____ / _____   TODAY'S MOOD RATING: 1 2 3 4 5

DAILY CLICHÉ: *Live and let live*

Who I said something nice to and what I said:

_____

_____

_____

Thoughts or feelings I had related to alcohol today:

How I feel today about being powerless over alcohol:

_____

_____

_____

I'm learning to accept or surrender:

A struggle I had and how I could have handled it better:

_____

_____

_____

_____

_____

What I did today to help make my life more manageable:

How I feel about my progress in recovery thus far:

TODAY'S ACTION LIST

Morning Prayer/Meditation ☑

Read Scripture/Recovery Lit ☑

Attended a Meeting ☑

Called Sponsor/Someone Sober ☑

Showered ☑   Teeth Brushed ☑

Water I Drank   1 2 3 4 5 6 7 8

Hours I Slept   1 2 3 4 5 6 7 8

TODAY'S GOALS

1. _____ ☑

2. _____ ☑

3. _____ ☑

TODAY'S PLANS	TIME

POSITIVE THINGS I DID TODAY

A REALIZATION OR CLARITY I HAD

TODAY I'M GRATEFUL FOR

Weekly Check-in

Week of: _____

WEEKLY MONTRA: *I am enough!*

| Do I see any trigger patterns? |

| Did I call my sponsor/counselor when I was triggered? |

| How my coping strategies worked last week: |

| Coping strategies I'll use this coming week: |

| Last week's biggest struggle: |

| How I'll overcome it this week: |

| Last week's biggest win: |

| How I'll keep it up moving forward: |

| What I learned about myself this week: |

MEETING DAYS	SOBER DAYS
Sunday ☑	☑ Sunday
Monday ☑	☐ Monday
Tuesday ☑	☐ Tuesday
Wednesday ☑	☐ Wednesday
Thursday ☑	☐ Thursday
Friday ☑	☑ Friday
Saturday ☑	☐ Saturday

THIS WEEK'S TOP GOALS

1. _____
2. _____
3. _____

HOW I'LL ACCOMPLISH THEM

_____
_____
_____
_____
_____
_____

TOOLS & HELP I'LL USE

_____
_____
_____

WHAT I CAN CELEBRATE & HOW

**ONE NEW COPING STRATEGY
I'LL TRY THIS WEEK**

Date: _____ / _____ / _____   TODAY'S MOOD RATING: 1 2 3 4 5

DAILY CLICHÉ: *Think, think, think*

Who I said something nice to and what I said:

_____
_____
_____

Thoughts or feelings I had related to alcohol today:

How I feel today about being powerless over alcohol:

_____
_____
_____

I'm learning to accept or surrender:

A struggle I had and how I could have handled it better:

_____
_____
_____
_____
_____

What I did today to help make my life more manageable:

How I feel about my progress in recovery thus far:

TODAY'S ACTION LIST

Morning Prayer/Meditation ☑

Read Scripture/Recovery Lit ☑

Attended a Meeting ☑

Called Sponsor/Someone Sober ☑

Showered ☑   Teeth Brushed ☑

Water I Drank   1 2 3 4 5 6 7 8

Hours I Slept   1 2 3 4 5 6 7 8

TODAY'S GOALS

1. _____ ☑

2. _____ ☑

3. _____ ☑

TODAY'S PLANS	TIME

POSITIVE THINGS I DID TODAY

A REALIZATION OR CLARITY I HAD

TODAY I'M GRATEFUL FOR

Date: _____ / _____ / _____   TODAY'S MOOD RATING: 1 2 3 4 5

DAILY CLICHÉ: *Keep it simple*

Who I said something nice to and what I said:

Thoughts or feelings I had related to alcohol today:

How I feel today about being powerless over alcohol:

I'm learning to accept or surrender:

A struggle I had and how I could have handled it better:

What I did today to help make my life more manageable:

How I feel about my progress in recovery thus far:

TODAY'S ACTION LIST

Morning Prayer/Meditation ☐
Read Scripture/Recovery Lit ☐
Attended a Meeting ☐
Called Sponsor/Someone Sober ☐
Showered ☐   Teeth Brushed ☐
Water I Drank   1 2 3 4 5 6 7 8
Hours I Slept   1 2 3 4 5 6 7 8

TODAY'S GOALS

1. _____ ☐
2. _____ ☐
3. _____ ☐

TODAY'S PLANS	TIME

POSITIVE THINGS I DID TODAY

A REALIZATION OR CLARITY I HAD

TODAY I'M GRATEFUL FOR

99

Date: _____ / _____ / _____   TODAY'S MOOD RATING: 1 2 3 4 5

DAILY CLICHÉ: *Find serenity in surrender*

Who I said something nice to and what I said:

Thoughts or feelings I had related to alcohol today:

How I feel today about being powerless over alcohol:

I'm learning to accept or surrender:

A struggle I had and how I could have handled it better:

What I did today to help make my life more manageable:

How I feel about my progress in recovery thus far:

TODAY'S ACTION LIST

Morning Prayer/Meditation ☑
Read Scripture/Recovery Lit ☑
Attended a Meeting ☑
Called Sponsor/Someone Sober ☑
Showered ☑   Teeth Brushed ☑
Water I Drank   1 2 3 4 5 6 7 8
Hours I Slept   1 2 3 4 5 6 7 8

TODAY'S GOALS

1. _____ ☐
2. _____ ☐
3. _____ ☐

TODAY'S PLANS	TIME

POSITIVE THINGS I DID TODAY

A REALIZATION OR CLARITY I HAD

TODAY I'M GRATEFUL FOR

Date: _____ / _____ / _____

TODAY'S MOOD RATING: 1 2 3 4 5

DAILY CLICHÉ:

Keep coming back

Who I said something nice to and what I said:

Thoughts or feelings I had related to alcohol today:

How I feel today about being powerless over alcohol:

I'm learning to accept or surrender:

A struggle I had and how I could have handled it better:

What I did today to help make my life more manageable:

How I feel about my progress in recovery thus far:

TODAY'S ACTION LIST

Morning Prayer/Meditation ☐

Read Scripture/Recovery Lit ☐

Attended a Meeting ☐

Called Sponsor/Someone Sober ☐

Showered ☐   Teeth Brushed ☐

Water I Drank   1 2 3 4 5 6 7 8

Hours I Slept   1 2 3 4 5 6 7 8

TODAY'S GOALS

1. _____ ☐

2. _____ ☐

3. _____ ☐

TODAY'S PLANS	TIME

POSITIVE THINGS I DID TODAY

A REALIZATION OR CLARITY I HAD

TODAY I'M GRATEFUL FOR

Date: _____ / _____ / _____

DAILY CLICHÉ:

Trust the process

TODAY'S MOOD RATING: 1 2 3 4 5

Who I said something nice to and what I said:

Thoughts or feelings I had related to alcohol today:

How I feel today about being powerless over alcohol:

I'm learning to accept or surrender:

A struggle I had and how I could have handled it better:

What I did today to help make my life more manageable:

How I feel about my progress in recovery thus far:

TODAY'S ACTION LIST
Morning Prayer/Meditation ☑
Read Scripture/Recovery Lit ☑
Attended a Meeting ☑
Called Sponsor/Someone Sober ☑
Showered ☑   Teeth Brushed ☑
Water I Drank   1 2 3 4 5 6 7 8
Hours I Slept   1 2 3 4 5 6 7 8

TODAY'S GOALS
1. _____ ☑
2. _____ ☑
3. _____ ☑

TODAY'S PLANS	TIME

POSITIVE THINGS I DID TODAY

A REALIZATION OR CLARITY I HAD

TODAY I'M GRATEFUL FOR

102

Date: _____ / _____ / _____   TODAY'S MOOD RATING: 1 2 3 4 5

DAILY CLICHÉ: *Live life on life's terms*

Who I said something nice to and what I said:

Thoughts or feelings I had related to alcohol today:

How I feel today about being powerless over alcohol:

I'm learning to accept or surrender:

A struggle I had and how I could have handled it better:

What I did today to help make my life more manageable:

How I feel about my progress in recovery thus far:

TODAY'S ACTION LIST

Morning Prayer/Meditation ☐
Read Scripture/Recovery Lit ☐
Attended a Meeting ☐
Called Sponsor/Someone Sober ☐
Showered ☐   Teeth Brushed ☐
Water I Drank   1 2 3 4 5 6 7 8
Hours I Slept   1 2 3 4 5 6 7 8

TODAY'S GOALS

1. _____ ☐
2. _____ ☐
3. _____ ☐

TODAY'S PLANS	TIME

POSITIVE THINGS I DID TODAY

A REALIZATION OR CLARITY I HAD

TODAY I'M GRATEFUL FOR

Date: _____ / _____ / _____   TODAY'S MOOD RATING: 1 2 3 4 5

DAILY CLICHÉ: *The only way out is through*

Who I said something nice to and what I said:

Thoughts or feelings I had related to alcohol today:

How I feel today about being powerless over alcohol:

I'm learning to accept or surrender:

A struggle I had and how I could have handled it better:

What I did today to help make my life more manageable:

How I feel about my progress in recovery thus far:

TODAY'S ACTION LIST
Morning Prayer/Meditation ☑
Read Scripture/Recovery Lit ☑
Attended a Meeting ☐
Called Sponsor/Someone Sober ☐
Showered ☑   Teeth Brushed ☑
Water I Drank   1 2 3 4 5 6 7 8
Hours I Slept   1 2 3 4 5 6 7 8

TODAY'S GOALS
1. _____ ☐
2. _____ ☐
3. _____ ☐

TODAY'S PLANS	TIME

POSITIVE THINGS I DID TODAY

A REALIZATION OR CLARITY I HAD

TODAY I'M GRATEFUL FOR

Weekly Check-in

Week of: _____

WEEKLY MONTRA: *I am strong and capable!*

Do I see any trigger patterns?

Did I call my sponsor/counselor when I was triggered?

How my coping strategies worked last week:

Coping strategies I'll use this coming week:

Last week's biggest struggle:

How I'll overcome it this week:

Last week's biggest win:

How I'll keep it up moving forward:

What I learned about myself this week:

MEETING DAYS	SOBER DAYS
Sunday ☑	☑ Sunday
Monday ☑	☑ Monday
Tuesday ☑	☑ Tuesday
Wednesday ☑	☑ Wednesday
Thursday ☑	☑ Thursday
Friday ☑	☑ Friday
Saturday ☑	☑ Saturday

THIS WEEK'S TOP GOALS

1. _____
2. _____
3. _____

HOW I'LL ACCOMPLISH THEM

TOOLS & HELP I'LL USE

WHAT I CAN CELEBRATE & HOW

ONE NEW COPING STRATEGY I'LL TRY THIS WEEK

Date: _____ / _____ / _____   TODAY'S MOOD RATING: 1 2 3 4 5

DAILY CLICHÉ: *Find the solution, not the blame*

Who I said something nice to and what I said:

_____
_____
_____

Thoughts or feelings I had related to alcohol today:

How I feel today about being powerless over alcohol:

_____
_____
_____

I'm learning to accept or surrender:

A struggle I had and how I could have handled it better:

_____
_____
_____
_____
_____

What I did today to help make my life more manageable:

How I feel about my progress in recovery thus far:

TODAY'S ACTION LIST
Morning Prayer/Meditation ☑

Read Scripture/Recovery Lit ☑

Attended a Meeting ☑

Called Sponsor/Someone Sober ☐

Showered ☑   Teeth Brushed ☑

Water I Drank   1 2 3 4 5 6 7 8

Hours I Slept   1 2 3 4 5 6 7 8

TODAY'S GOALS
1. _____ ☐
2. _____ ☐
3. _____ ☐

TODAY'S PLANS	TIME

POSITIVE THINGS I DID TODAY

A REALIZATION OR CLARITY I HAD

TODAY I'M GRATEFUL FOR

Date: _____ / _____ / _____   TODAY'S MOOD RATING: 1 2 3 4 5

DAILY CLICHÉ: *Progress, not perfection*

Who I said something nice to and what I said:

Thoughts or feelings I had related to alcohol today:

How I feel today about being powerless over alcohol:

I'm learning to accept or surrender:

A struggle I had and how I could have handled it better:

What I did today to help make my life more manageable:

How I feel about my progress in recovery thus far:

TODAY'S ACTION LIST

Morning Prayer/Meditation ☐
Read Scripture/Recovery Lit ☐
Attended a Meeting ☐
Called Sponsor/Someone Sober ☐
Showered ☐   Teeth Brushed ☐
Water I Drank   1 2 3 4 5 6 7 8
Hours I Slept   1 2 3 4 5 6 7 8

TODAY'S GOALS

1. _____ ☐
2. _____ ☐
3. _____ ☐

TODAY'S PLANS	TIME

POSITIVE THINGS I DID TODAY

A REALIZATION OR CLARITY I HAD

TODAY I'M GRATEFUL FOR

Date: _____ / _____ / _____   TODAY'S MOOD RATING: 1 2 3 4 5

DAILY CLICHÉ: *The solution is in the rooms*

Who I said something nice to and what I said:

Thoughts or feelings I had related to alcohol today:

How I feel today about being powerless over alcohol:

I'm learning to accept or surrender:

A struggle I had and how I could have handled it better:

What I did today to help make my life more manageable:

How I feel about my progress in recovery thus far:

TODAY'S ACTION LIST

Morning Prayer/Meditation ☑
Read Scripture/Recovery Lit ☑
Attended a Meeting ☑
Called Sponsor/Someone Sober ☑
Showered ☑   Teeth Brushed ☑
Water I Drank   1 2 3 4 5 6 7 8
Hours I Slept   1 2 3 4 5 6 7 8

TODAY'S GOALS

1. _____ ☐
2. _____ ☐
3. _____ ☐

TODAY'S PLANS	TIME

POSITIVE THINGS I DID TODAY

A REALIZATION OR CLARITY I HAD

TODAY I'M GRATEFUL FOR

Date: _____ / _____ / _____   TODAY'S MOOD RATING: 1 2 3 4 5

DAILY CLICHÉ: *Be willing*

Who I said something nice to and what I said:

Thoughts or feelings I had related to alcohol today:

How I feel today about being powerless over alcohol:

I'm learning to accept or surrender:

A struggle I had and how I could have handled it better:

What I did today to help make my life more manageable:

How I feel about my progress in recovery thus far:

TODAY'S ACTION LIST

Morning Prayer/Meditation ☑
Read Scripture/Recovery Lit ☑
Attended a Meeting ☑
Called Sponsor/Someone Sober ☑
Showered ☑   Teeth Brushed ☑
Water I Drank   1 2 3 4 5 6 7 8
Hours I Slept   1 2 3 4 5 6 7 8

TODAY'S GOALS

1. _____ ☑
2. _____ ☑
3. _____ ☑

TODAY'S PLANS	TIME

POSITIVE THINGS I DID TODAY

A REALIZATION OR CLARITY I HAD

TODAY I'M GRATEFUL FOR

Date: _____ / _____ / _____   TODAY'S MOOD RATING: 1 2 3 4 5

DAILY CLICHÉ: *Just for today*

Who I said something nice to and what I said:

Thoughts or feelings I had related to alcohol today:

How I feel today about being powerless over alcohol:

I'm learning to accept or surrender:

A struggle I had and how I could have handled it better:

What I did today to help make my life more manageable:

How I feel about my progress in recovery thus far:

TODAY'S ACTION LIST

Morning Prayer/Meditation ☑
Read Scripture/Recovery Lit ☑
Attended a Meeting ☑
Called Sponsor/Someone Sober ☐
Showered ☑   Teeth Brushed ☑
Water I Drank   1 2 3 4 5 6 7 8
Hours I Slept   1 2 3 4 5 6 7 8

TODAY'S GOALS

1. _____ ☑
2. _____ ☑
3. _____ ☑

TODAY'S PLANS	TIME

POSITIVE THINGS I DID TODAY

A REALIZATION OR CLARITY I HAD

TODAY I'M GRATEFUL FOR

Date: _____ / _____ / _____   TODAY'S MOOD RATING: 1 2 3 4 5

DAILY CLICHÉ: *Take the next right step*

Who I said something nice to and what I said:

Thoughts or feelings I had related to alcohol today:

How I feel today about being powerless over alcohol:

I'm learning to accept or surrender:

A struggle I had and how I could have handled it better:

What I did today to help make my life more manageable:

How I feel about my progress in recovery thus far:

TODAY'S ACTION LIST

Morning Prayer/Meditation ☑
Read Scripture/Recovery Lit ☑
Attended a Meeting ☑
Called Sponsor/Someone Sober ☑
Showered ☑   Teeth Brushed ☑
Water I Drank   1 2 3 4 5 6 7 8
Hours I Slept   1 2 3 4 5 6 7 8

TODAY'S GOALS

1. _____ ☐
2. _____ ☐
3. _____ ☐

TODAY'S PLANS	TIME

POSITIVE THINGS I DID TODAY

A REALIZATION OR CLARITY I HAD

TODAY I'M GRATEFUL FOR

Date: _____ / _____ / _____   TODAY'S MOOD RATING: 1 2 3 4 5

DAILY CLICHÉ: *Stay right sized*

Who I said something nice to and what I said:
_____
_____
_____

Thoughts or feelings I had related to alcohol today:

How I feel today about being powerless over alcohol:
_____
_____
_____

I'm learning to accept or surrender:

A struggle I had and how I could have handled it better:
_____
_____
_____
_____
_____

What I did today to help make my life more manageable:

How I feel about my progress in recovery thus far:

TODAY'S ACTION LIST

Morning Prayer/Meditation ☑
Read Scripture/Recovery Lit ☑
Attended a Meeting ☑
Called Sponsor/Someone Sober ☐
Showered ☑   Teeth Brushed ☑
Water I Drank   1 2 3 4 5 6 7 8
Hours I Slept   1 2 3 4 5 6 7 8

TODAY'S GOALS

1. _____ ☐
2. _____ ☐
3. _____ ☐

TODAY'S PLANS	TIME

POSITIVE THINGS I DID TODAY

A REALIZATION OR CLARITY I HAD

TODAY I'M GRATEFUL FOR

Weekly Check-in

Week of: _____

WEEKLY MONTRA: *I choose to focus on the positive!*

Do I see any trigger patterns?

Did I call my sponsor/counselor when I was triggered?

How my coping strategies worked last week:

Coping strategies I'll use this coming week:

Last week's biggest struggle:

How I'll overcome it this week:

Last week's biggest win:

How I'll keep it up moving forward:

What I learned about myself this week:

MEETING DAYS	SOBER DAYS
Sunday ☑	☑ Sunday
Monday ☑	☑ Monday
Tuesday ☑	☑ Tuesday
Wednesday ☑	☑ Wednesday
Thursday ☑	☑ Thursday
Friday ☑	☑ Friday
Saturday ☑	☑ Saturday

THIS WEEK'S TOP GOALS

1. _____
2. _____
3. _____

HOW I'LL ACCOMPLISH THEM

TOOLS & HELP I'LL USE

WHAT I CAN CELEBRATE & HOW

**ONE NEW COPING STRATEGY
I'LL TRY THIS WEEK**

Date: _____ / _____ / _____   TODAY'S MOOD RATING: 1 2 3 4 5

DAILY CLICHÉ: *Get out of your own way*

Who I said something nice to and what I said:

Thoughts or feelings I had related to alcohol today:

How I feel today about being powerless over alcohol:

I'm learning to accept or surrender:

A struggle I had and how I could have handled it better:

What I did today to help make my life more manageable:

How I feel about my progress in recovery thus far:

TODAY'S ACTION LIST
Morning Prayer/Meditation ☑

Read Scripture/Recovery Lit ☑

Attended a Meeting ☑

Called Sponsor/Someone Sober ☑

Showered ☑   Teeth Brushed ☑

Water I Drank   1 2 3 4 5 6 7 8

Hours I Slept   1 2 3 4 5 6 7 8

TODAY'S GOALS

1. _____ ☐

2. _____ ☐

3. _____ ☐

TODAY'S PLANS	TIME

POSITIVE THINGS I DID TODAY

A REALIZATION OR CLARITY I HAD

TODAY I'M GRATEFUL FOR

Date: _____ / _____ / _____   TODAY'S MOOD RATING: 1 2 3 4 5

DAILY CLICHÉ: *Do the next right thing*

Who I said something nice to and what I said:

Thoughts or feelings I had related to alcohol today:

How I feel today about being powerless over alcohol:

I'm learning to accept or surrender:

A struggle I had and how I could have handled it better:

What I did today to help make my life more manageable:

How I feel about my progress in recovery thus far:

TODAY'S ACTION LIST

Morning Prayer/Meditation ☐
Read Scripture/Recovery Lit ☐
Attended a Meeting ☐
Called Sponsor/Someone Sober ☐
Showered ☐   Teeth Brushed ☐
Water I Drank   1 2 3 4 5 6 7 8
Hours I Slept   1 2 3 4 5 6 7 8

TODAY'S GOALS

1. _____ ☐
2. _____ ☐
3. _____ ☐

TODAY'S PLANS	TIME

POSITIVE THINGS I DID TODAY

A REALIZATION OR CLARITY I HAD

TODAY I'M GRATEFUL FOR

Date: _____ / _____ / _____   TODAY'S MOOD RATING: 1 2 3 4 5

DAILY CLICHÉ: *Acceptance is the answer*

Who I said something nice to and what I said:

_____
_____
_____

Thoughts or feelings I had related to alcohol today:

How I feel today about being powerless over alcohol:

_____
_____
_____

I'm learning to accept or surrender:

A struggle I had and how I could have handled it better:

_____
_____
_____
_____

What I did today to help make my life more manageable:

How I feel about my progress in recovery thus far:

TODAY'S ACTION LIST

Morning Prayer/Meditation ☑
Read Scripture/Recovery Lit ☑
Attended a Meeting ☑
Called Sponsor/Someone Sober ☑
Showered ☑   Teeth Brushed ☑
Water I Drank   1 2 3 4 5 6 7 8
Hours I Slept   1 2 3 4 5 6 7 8

TODAY'S GOALS

1. _____ ☐
2. _____ ☐
3. _____ ☐

TODAY'S PLANS	TIME

POSITIVE THINGS I DID TODAY

A REALIZATION OR CLARITY I HAD

TODAY I'M GRATEFUL FOR

Date: _____ / _____ / _____   TODAY'S MOOD RATING: 1 2 3 4 5

DAILY CLICHÉ: *Practice the principles*

Who I said something nice to and what I said:

Thoughts or feelings I had related to alcohol today:

How I feel today about being powerless over alcohol:

I'm learning to accept or surrender:

A struggle I had and how I could have handled it better:

What I did today to help make my life more manageable:

How I feel about my progress in recovery thus far:

TODAY'S ACTION LIST

Morning Prayer/Meditation ☐
Read Scripture/Recovery Lit ☐
Attended a Meeting ☐
Called Sponsor/Someone Sober ☐
Showered ☐   Teeth Brushed ☐
Water I Drank   1 2 3 4 5 6 7 8
Hours I Slept   1 2 3 4 5 6 7 8

TODAY'S GOALS

1. _____ ☐
2. _____ ☐
3. _____ ☐

TODAY'S PLANS	TIME

POSITIVE THINGS I DID TODAY

A REALIZATION OR CLARITY I HAD

TODAY I'M GRATEFUL FOR

Date: _____ / _____ / _____   TODAY'S MOOD RATING: 1 2 3 4 5

DAILY CLICHÉ: *Focus on what you can control*

Who I said something nice to and what I said:

_____
_____
_____

Thoughts or feelings I had related to alcohol today:

How I feel today about being powerless over alcohol:

_____
_____
_____

I'm learning to accept or surrender:

A struggle I had and how I could have handled it better:

_____
_____
_____
_____
_____

What I did today to help make my life more manageable:

How I feel about my progress in recovery thus far:

TODAY'S ACTION LIST

Morning Prayer/Meditation ☐
Read Scripture/Recovery Lit ☐
Attended a Meeting ☐
Called Sponsor/Someone Sober ☐
Showered ☐   Teeth Brushed ☐
Water I Drank   1 2 3 4 5 6 7 8
Hours I Slept   1 2 3 4 5 6 7 8

TODAY'S GOALS

1. _____ ☐
2. _____ ☐
3. _____ ☐

TODAY'S PLANS	TIME

POSITIVE THINGS I DID TODAY

A REALIZATION OR CLARITY I HAD

TODAY I'M GRATEFUL FOR

Date: _____ / _____ / _____   TODAY'S MOOD RATING: 1 2 3 4 5

DAILY CLICHÉ: *Let gratitude be your attitude*

Who I said something nice to and what I said:

Thoughts or feelings I had related to alcohol today:

How I feel today about being powerless over alcohol:

I'm learning to accept or surrender:

A struggle I had and how I could have handled it better:

What I did today to help make my life more manageable:

How I feel about my progress in recovery thus far:

TODAY'S ACTION LIST

Morning Prayer/Meditation ☐
Read Scripture/Recovery Lit ☐
Attended a Meeting ☐
Called Sponsor/Someone Sober ☐
Showered ☐   Teeth Brushed ☐
Water I Drank   1 2 3 4 5 6 7 8
Hours I Slept   1 2 3 4 5 6 7 8

TODAY'S GOALS

1. _____ ☐
2. _____ ☐
3. _____ ☐

TODAY'S PLANS	TIME

POSITIVE THINGS I DID TODAY

A REALIZATION OR CLARITY I HAD

TODAY I'M GRATEFUL FOR

Date: _____ / _____ / _____   TODAY'S MOOD RATING: 1 2 3 4 5

DAILY CLICHÉ: *Let your higher power do the heavy lifting*

Who I said something nice to and what I said:

Thoughts or feelings I had related to alcohol today:

How I feel today about being powerless over alcohol:

I'm learning to accept or surrender:

A struggle I had and how I could have handled it better:

What I did today to help make my life more manageable:

How I feel about my progress in recovery thus far:

TODAY'S ACTION LIST

Morning Prayer/Meditation ☑

Read Scripture/Recovery Lit ☑

Attended a Meeting ☑

Called Sponsor/Someone Sober ☑

Showered ☑   Teeth Brushed ☑

Water I Drank   1 2 3 4 5 6 7 8

Hours I Slept   1 2 3 4 5 6 7 8

TODAY'S GOALS

1. _____ ☐

2. _____ ☐

3. _____ ☐

TODAY'S PLANS	TIME

POSITIVE THINGS I DID TODAY

A REALIZATION OR CLARITY I HAD

TODAY I'M GRATEFUL FOR

Weekly Check-in

Week of: _____

WEEKLY MONTRA: *I am worthy of love!*

Do I see any trigger patterns?

Did I call my sponsor/counselor when I was triggered?

How my coping strategies worked last week:

Coping strategies I'll use this coming week:

Last week's biggest struggle:

How I'll overcome it this week:

Last week's biggest win:

How I'll keep it up moving forward:

What I learned about myself this week:

MEETING DAYS	SOBER DAYS
Sunday ☑	☑ Sunday
Monday ☑	☑ Monday
Tuesday ☑	☑ Tuesday
Wednesday ☑	☑ Wednesday
Thursday ☑	☑ Thursday
Friday ☑	☑ Friday
Saturday ☑	☑ Saturday

THIS WEEK'S TOP GOALS

1. _____
2. _____
3. _____

HOW I'LL ACCOMPLISH THEM

TOOLS & HELP I'LL USE

WHAT I CAN CELEBRATE & HOW

ONE NEW COPING STRATEGY I'LL TRY THIS WEEK

Date: _____ / _____ / _____   TODAY'S MOOD RATING: 1 2 3 4 5

DAILY CLICHÉ: *Let go of perfection*

Who I said something nice to and what I said:

_____
_____
_____

Thoughts or feelings I had related to alcohol today:

How I feel today about being powerless over alcohol:

_____
_____
_____

I'm learning to accept or surrender:

A struggle I had and how I could have handled it better:

_____
_____
_____
_____
_____

What I did today to help make my life more manageable:

How I feel about my progress in recovery thus far:

TODAY'S ACTION LIST

Morning Prayer/Meditation ☑
Read Scripture/Recovery Lit ☑
Attended a Meeting ☑
Called Sponsor/Someone Sober ☐
Showered ☑   Teeth Brushed ☑
Water I Drank   1 2 3 4 5 6 7 8
Hours I Slept   1 2 3 4 5 6 7 8

TODAY'S GOALS

1. _____ ☐
2. _____ ☐
3. _____ ☐

TODAY'S PLANS	TIME

POSITIVE THINGS I DID TODAY

A REALIZATION OR CLARITY I HAD

TODAY I'M GRATEFUL FOR

122

Date: _____ / _____ / _____   TODAY'S MOOD RATING: 1 2 3 4 5

DAILY CLICHÉ: *Turn it over*

Who I said something nice to and what I said:

Thoughts or feelings I had related to alcohol today:

How I feel today about being powerless over alcohol:

I'm learning to accept or surrender:

A struggle I had and how I could have handled it better:

What I did today to help make my life more manageable:

How I feel about my progress in recovery thus far:

TODAY'S ACTION LIST

Morning Prayer/Meditation ☐
Read Scripture/Recovery Lit ☐
Attended a Meeting ☐
Called Sponsor/Someone Sober ☐
Showered ☐   Teeth Brushed ☐
Water I Drank   1 2 3 4 5 6 7 8
Hours I Slept   1 2 3 4 5 6 7 8

TODAY'S GOALS

1. _____ ☐
2. _____ ☐
3. _____ ☐

TODAY'S PLANS	TIME

POSITIVE THINGS I DID TODAY

A REALIZATION OR CLARITY I HAD

TODAY I'M GRATEFUL FOR

Date: _____ / _____ / _____   TODAY'S MOOD RATING: 1 2 3 4 5

DAILY CLICHÉ: *Fake it till you make it*

Who I said something nice to and what I said:

Thoughts or feelings I had related to alcohol today:

How I feel today about being powerless over alcohol:

I'm learning to accept or surrender:

A struggle I had and how I could have handled it better:

What I did today to help make my life more manageable:

How I feel about my progress in recovery thus far:

TODAY'S ACTION LIST

Morning Prayer/Meditation ☑
Read Scripture/Recovery Lit ☑
Attended a Meeting ☑
Called Sponsor/Someone Sober ☑
Showered ☑   Teeth Brushed ☑
Water I Drank   1 2 3 4 5 6 7 8
Hours I Slept   1 2 3 4 5 6 7 8

TODAY'S GOALS

1. _____ ☐
2. _____ ☐
3. _____ ☐

TODAY'S PLANS	TIME

POSITIVE THINGS I DID TODAY

A REALIZATION OR CLARITY I HAD

TODAY I'M GRATEFUL FOR

Date: _____ / _____ / _____   TODAY'S MOOD RATING: 1 2 3 4 5

DAILY CLICHÉ: *One step at a time*

Who I said something nice to and what I said:

Thoughts or feelings I had related to alcohol today:

How I feel today about being powerless over alcohol:

I'm learning to accept or surrender:

A struggle I had and how I could have handled it better:

What I did today to help make my life more manageable:

How I feel about my progress in recovery thus far:

TODAY'S ACTION LIST

Morning Prayer/Meditation ☐
Read Scripture/Recovery Lit ☐
Attended a Meeting ☐
Called Sponsor/Someone Sober ☐
Showered ☐   Teeth Brushed ☐
Water I Drank   1 2 3 4 5 6 7 8
Hours I Slept   1 2 3 4 5 6 7 8

TODAY'S GOALS

1. _____ ☐
2. _____ ☐
3. _____ ☐

TODAY'S PLANS	TIME

POSITIVE THINGS I DID TODAY

A REALIZATION OR CLARITY I HAD

TODAY I'M GRATEFUL FOR

Date: _____ / _____ / _____   TODAY'S MOOD RATING: 1 2 3 4 5

DAILY CLICHÉ: *We're only as sick as our secrets*

Who I said something nice to and what I said:

Thoughts or feelings I had related to alcohol today:

How I feel today about being powerless over alcohol:

I'm learning to accept or surrender:

A struggle I had and how I could have handled it better:

What I did today to help make my life more manageable:

How I feel about my progress in recovery thus far:

TODAY'S ACTION LIST
Morning Prayer/Meditation ☑
Read Scripture/Recovery Lit ☑
Attended a Meeting ☑
Called Sponsor/Someone Sober ☑
Showered ☑   Teeth Brushed ☑
Water I Drank   1 2 3 4 5 6 7 8
Hours I Slept   1 2 3 4 5 6 7 8

TODAY'S GOALS
1. _____ ☐
2. _____ ☐
3. _____ ☐

TODAY'S PLANS	TIME

POSITIVE THINGS I DID TODAY

A REALIZATION OR CLARITY I HAD

TODAY I'M GRATEFUL FOR

126

Date: _____ / _____ / _____   TODAY'S MOOD RATING: 1 2 3 4 5

DAILY CLICHÉ: *You're not alone*

Who I said something nice to and what I said:

Thoughts or feelings I had related to alcohol today:

How I feel today about being powerless over alcohol:

I'm learning to accept or surrender:

A struggle I had and how I could have handled it better:

What I did today to help make my life more manageable:

How I feel about my progress in recovery thus far:

TODAY'S ACTION LIST

Morning Prayer/Meditation ☐
Read Scripture/Recovery Lit ☐
Attended a Meeting ☐
Called Sponsor/Someone Sober ☐
Showered ☐   Teeth Brushed ☐
Water I Drank   1 2 3 4 5 6 7 8
Hours I Slept   1 2 3 4 5 6 7 8

TODAY'S GOALS

1. _____ ☐
2. _____ ☐
3. _____ ☐

TODAY'S PLANS	TIME

POSITIVE THINGS I DID TODAY

A REALIZATION OR CLARITY I HAD

TODAY I'M GRATEFUL FOR

Date: _____ / _____ / _____   TODAY'S MOOD RATING: 1 2 3 4 5

DAILY CLICHÉ: *There's a solution*

Who I said something nice to and what I said:

Thoughts or feelings I had related to alcohol today:

How I feel today about being powerless over alcohol:

I'm learning to accept or surrender:

A struggle I had and how I could have handled it better:

What I did today to help make my life more manageable:

How I feel about my progress in recovery thus far:

TODAY'S ACTION LIST

Morning Prayer/Meditation ☑

Read Scripture/Recovery Lit ☑

Attended a Meeting ☑

Called Sponsor/Someone Sober ☑

Showered ☑   Teeth Brushed ☑

Water I Drank   1 2 3 4 5 6 7 8

Hours I Slept   1 2 3 4 5 6 7 8

TODAY'S GOALS

1. _____ ☑
2. _____ ☑
3. _____ ☑

TODAY'S PLANS	TIME

POSITIVE THINGS I DID TODAY

A REALIZATION OR CLARITY I HAD

TODAY I'M GRATEFUL FOR

Weekly Check-in

Week of: _____

WEEKLY MONTRA: *I am worthy of happiness!*

Do I see any trigger patterns?

Did I call my sponsor/counselor when I was triggered?

How my coping strategies worked last week:

Coping strategies I'll use this coming week:

Last week's biggest struggle:

How I'll overcome it this week:

Last week's biggest win:

How I'll keep it up moving forward:

What I learned about myself this week:

MEETING DAYS	SOBER DAYS
Sunday ☑	☑ Sunday
Monday ☑	☑ Monday
Tuesday ☑	☑ Tuesday
Wednesday ☑	☑ Wednesday
Thursday ☑	☑ Thursday
Friday ☑	☑ Friday
Saturday ☑	☑ Saturday

THIS WEEK'S TOP GOALS

1. _____
2. _____
3. _____

HOW I'LL ACCOMPLISH THEM

TOOLS & HELP I'LL USE

WHAT I CAN CELEBRATE & HOW

ONE NEW COPING STRATEGY I'LL TRY THIS WEEK

Date: _____ / _____ / _____   TODAY'S MOOD RATING: 1 2 3 4 5

DAILY CLICHÉ: *Sobriety is a journey, not a destination*

Who I said something nice to and what I said:
_____
_____
_____
_____

Thoughts or feelings I had related to alcohol today:
_____
_____

How I feel today about being powerless over alcohol:
_____
_____
_____
_____

I'm learning to accept or surrender:
_____
_____

A struggle I had and how I could have handled it better:
_____
_____
_____
_____
_____
_____
_____

What I did today to help make my life more manageable:
_____
_____

How I feel about my progress in recovery thus far:

TODAY'S ACTION LIST	
Morning Prayer/Meditation	☑
Read Scripture/Recovery Lit	☑
Attended a Meeting	☑
Called Sponsor/Someone Sober	☑
Showered ☑ Teeth Brushed	☑

Water I Drank   1 2 3 4 5 6 7 8
Hours I Slept   1 2 3 4 5 6 7 8

TODAY'S GOALS

1. _____ ☑
2. _____ ☑
3. _____ ☑

TODAY'S PLANS	TIME

POSITIVE THINGS I DID TODAY
_____
_____
_____
_____

A REALIZATION OR CLARITY I HAD

TODAY I'M GRATEFUL FOR

Date: _____ / _____ / _____   TODAY'S MOOD RATING: 1 2 3 4 5

DAILY CLICHÉ: *Take what you need, leave the rest*

Who I said something nice to and what I said:
_____
_____
_____

Thoughts or feelings I had related to alcohol today:

How I feel today about being powerless over alcohol:
_____
_____
_____

I'm learning to accept or surrender:

A struggle I had and how I could have handled it better:
_____
_____
_____
_____
_____

What I did today to help make my life more manageable:

How I feel about my progress in recovery thus far:

TODAY'S ACTION LIST

Morning Prayer/Meditation ☑
Read Scripture/Recovery Lit ☑
Attended a Meeting ☑
Called Sponsor/Someone Sober ☑
Showered ☑   Teeth Brushed ☑
Water I Drank   1 2 3 4 5 6 7 8
Hours I Slept   1 2 3 4 5 6 7 8

TODAY'S GOALS

1. _____ ☐
2. _____ ☐
3. _____ ☐

TODAY'S PLANS	TIME

POSITIVE THINGS I DID TODAY

A REALIZATION OR CLARITY I HAD

TODAY I'M GRATEFUL FOR

Date: _____ / _____ / _____   TODAY'S MOOD RATING: 1 2 3 4 5

DAILY CLICHÉ: *Nothing changes if nothing changes*

Who I said something nice to and what I said:
_____
_____
_____

Thoughts or feelings I had related to alcohol today:

How I feel today about being powerless over alcohol:
_____
_____
_____

I'm learning to accept or surrender:

A struggle I had and how I could have handled it better:
_____
_____
_____
_____
_____
_____

What I did today to help make my life more manageable:

How I feel about my progress in recovery thus far:

TODAY'S ACTION LIST

Morning Prayer/Meditation ☑
Read Scripture/Recovery Lit ☑
Attended a Meeting ☑
Called Sponsor/Someone Sober ☑
Showered ☑   Teeth Brushed ☑
Water I Drank   1 2 3 4 5 6 7 8
Hours I Slept   1 2 3 4 5 6 7 8

TODAY'S GOALS

1. _____ ☑
2. _____ ☑
3. _____ ☑

TODAY'S PLANS	TIME

POSITIVE THINGS I DID TODAY

A REALIZATION OR CLARITY I HAD

TODAY I'M GRATEFUL FOR

132

Date: _____ / _____ / _____   TODAY'S MOOD RATING: 1 2 3 4 5

DAILY CLICHÉ: *Don't quit 15 minutes before the miracle happens*

Who I said something nice to and what I said:

Thoughts or feelings I had related to alcohol today:

How I feel today about being powerless over alcohol:

I'm learning to accept or surrender:

A struggle I had and how I could have handled it better:

What I did today to help make my life more manageable:

How I feel about my progress in recovery thus far:

TODAY'S ACTION LIST

Morning Prayer/Meditation ☐
Read Scripture/Recovery Lit ☐
Attended a Meeting ☐
Called Sponsor/Someone Sober ☐
Showered ☐   Teeth Brushed ☐
Water I Drank   1 2 3 4 5 6 7 8
Hours I Slept   1 2 3 4 5 6 7 8

TODAY'S GOALS

1. _____ ☐
2. _____ ☐
3. _____ ☐

TODAY'S PLANS	TIME

POSITIVE THINGS I DID TODAY

A REALIZATION OR CLARITY I HAD

TODAY I'M GRATEFUL FOR

Date: _____ / _____ / _____   TODAY'S MOOD RATING: 1 2 3 4 5

DAILY CLICHÉ: *Accept your admission*

Who I said something nice to and what I said:
_____
_____
_____

Thoughts or feelings I had related to alcohol today:

How I feel today about being powerless over alcohol:
_____
_____
_____
_____

I'm learning to accept or surrender:

A struggle I had and how I could have handled it better:
_____
_____
_____
_____
_____
_____

What I did today to help make my life more manageable:

How I feel about my progress in recovery thus far:

TODAY'S ACTION LIST

Morning Prayer/Meditation ☑

Read Scripture/Recovery Lit ☑

Attended a Meeting ☑

Called Sponsor/Someone Sober ☑

Showered ☑   Teeth Brushed ☑

Water I Drank   1 2 3 4 5 6 7 8

Hours I Slept   1 2 3 4 5 6 7 8

TODAY'S GOALS

1. _____ ☑

2. _____ ☑

3. _____ ☑

TODAY'S PLANS	TIME

POSITIVE THINGS I DID TODAY

A REALIZATION OR CLARITY I HAD

TODAY I'M GRATEFUL FOR

Date: _____ / _____ / _____   TODAY'S MOOD RATING: 1 2 3 4 5

DAILY CLICHÉ: *Courage to change*

Who I said something nice to and what I said:

Thoughts or feelings I had related to alcohol today:

How I feel today about being powerless over alcohol:

I'm learning to accept or surrender:

A struggle I had and how I could have handled it better:

What I did today to help make my life more manageable:

How I feel about my progress in recovery thus far:

TODAY'S ACTION LIST

Morning Prayer/Meditation ☐
Read Scripture/Recovery Lit ☐
Attended a Meeting ☐
Called Sponsor/Someone Sober ☐
Showered ☐   Teeth Brushed ☐
Water I Drank   1 2 3 4 5 6 7 8
Hours I Slept   1 2 3 4 5 6 7 8

TODAY'S GOALS

1. _____ ☐
2. _____ ☐
3. _____ ☐

TODAY'S PLANS	TIME

POSITIVE THINGS I DID TODAY

A REALIZATION OR CLARITY I HAD

TODAY I'M GRATEFUL FOR

Date: _____ / _____ / _____   TODAY'S MOOD RATING: 1 2 3 4 5

DAILY CLICHÉ: *The journey of a thousand miles begins with a single step*

Who I said something nice to and what I said:

Thoughts or feelings I had related to alcohol today:

How I feel today about being powerless over alcohol:

I'm learning to accept or surrender:

A struggle I had and how I could have handled it better:

What I did today to help make my life more manageable:

How I feel about my progress in recovery thus far:

TODAY'S ACTION LIST
Morning Prayer/Meditation ☑
Read Scripture/Recovery Lit ☑
Attended a Meeting ☑
Called Sponsor/Someone Sober ☑
Showered ☑   Teeth Brushed ☑
Water I Drank   1 2 3 4 5 6 7 8
Hours I Slept   1 2 3 4 5 6 7 8

TODAY'S GOALS
1. _____ ☐
2. _____ ☐
3. _____ ☐

TODAY'S PLANS	TIME

POSITIVE THINGS I DID TODAY

A REALIZATION OR CLARITY I HAD

TODAY I'M GRATEFUL FOR

Weekly Check-in

Week of: _____

WEEKLY MONTRA: *I am capable!*

Do I see any trigger patterns?

Did I call my sponsor/counselor when I was triggered?

How my coping strategies worked last week:

Coping strategies I'll use this coming week:

Last week's biggest struggle:

How I'll overcome it this week:

Last week's biggest win:

How I'll keep it up moving forward:

What I learned about myself this week:

MEETING DAYS	SOBER DAYS
Sunday ☑	☑ Sunday
Monday ☑	☑ Monday
Tuesday ☑	☑ Tuesday
Wednesday ☑	☑ Wednesday
Thursday ☑	☑ Thursday
Friday ☑	☑ Friday
Saturday ☑	☑ Saturday

THIS WEEK'S TOP GOALS

1. _____
2. _____
3. _____

HOW I'LL ACCOMPLISH THEM

_____
_____
_____
_____
_____
_____
_____
_____

TOOLS & HELP I'LL USE

_____
_____
_____

WHAT I CAN CELEBRATE & HOW

**ONE NEW COPING STRATEGY
I'LL TRY THIS WEEK**

Organization Contacts

ORGANIZATION1

Organization: _____ Contact Name: _____

Phone # _____ Cel #: _____

Web: _____ Email: _____

Address: _____

City: _____ State: _____ Zip: _____

Notes: _____

ORGANIZATION 2

Organization: _____ Contact Name: _____

Phone # _____ Cell #: _____

Web: _____ Email: _____

Address: _____

City: _____ State: _____ Zip: _____

Notes: _____

ORGANIZATION 3

Organization: _____ Contact Name: _____

Phone # _____ Cell #: _____

Web: _____ Email: _____

Address: _____

City: _____ State: _____ Zip: _____

Notes: _____

ORGANIZATION 4

Organization: _____ Contact Name: _____

Phone # _____ Cel #l: _____

Web: _____ Email: _____

Address: _____

City: _____ State: _____ Zip: _____

Notes: _____

ORGANIZATION 5

Organization: _____ Contact Name: _____

Phone # _____ Cell #: _____

Web: _____ Email: _____

Address: _____

City: _____ State: _____ Zip: _____

Notes: _____

Meeting Contacts

CONTACT 1

Name: _____ Email: _____
Phone # _____ Cell #: _____
Address: _____
City: _____ State: _____ Zip: _____
Notes: _____

CONTACT 2

Name: _____ Email: _____
Phone # _____ Cell #: _____
Address: _____
City: _____ State: _____ Zip: _____
Notes: _____

CONTACT 3

Name: _____ Email: _____
Phone # _____ Cell #: _____
Address: _____
City: _____ State: _____ Zip: _____
Notes: _____

CONTACT 4

Name: _____ Email: _____
Phone # _____ Cell #: _____
Address: _____
City: _____ State: _____ Zip: _____
Notes: _____

CONTACT 5

Name: _____ Email: _____
Phone # _____ Cell #: _____
Address: _____
City: _____ State: _____ Zip: _____
Notes: _____

CONTACT 6

Name: _____ Email: _____
Phone # _____ Cell #: _____
Address: _____
City: _____ State: _____ Zip: _____
Notes: _____

Meeting Contacts

CONTACT 7

Name: _____ Email: _____
Phone # _____ Cell #: _____
Address: _____
City: _____ State: _____ Zip: _____
Notes: _____

CONTACT 8

Name: _____ Email: _____
Phone # _____ Cell #: _____
Address: _____
City: _____ State: _____ Zip: _____
Notes: _____

CONTACT 9

Name: _____ Email: _____
Phone # _____ Cell #: _____
Address: _____
City: _____ State: _____ Zip: _____
Notes: _____

CONTACT 10

Name: _____ Email: _____
Phone # _____ Cell #: _____
Address: _____
City: _____ State: _____ Zip: _____
Notes: _____

CONTACT 11

Name: _____ Email: _____
Phone # _____ Cell #: _____
Address: _____
City: _____ State: _____ Zip: _____
Notes: _____

CONTACT 12

Name: _____ Email: _____
Phone # _____ Cell #: _____
Address: _____
City: _____ State: _____ Zip: _____
Notes: _____

Personal Contacts

CONTACT 1
Name: _____ Email: _____
Phone # _____ Cell #: _____
Address: _____
City: _____ State: _____ Zip: _____
Notes: _____

CONTACT 2
Name: _____ Email: _____
Phone # _____ Cell #: _____
Address: _____
City: _____ State: _____ Zip: _____
Notes: _____

CONTACT 3
Name: _____ Email: _____
Phone # _____ Cell #: _____
Address: _____
City: _____ State: _____ Zip: _____
Notes: _____

CONTACT 4
Name: _____ Email: _____
Phone # _____ Cell #: _____
Address: _____
City: _____ State: _____ Zip: _____
Notes: _____

CONTACT 5
Name: _____ Email: _____
Phone # _____ Cell #: _____
Address: _____
City: _____ State: _____ Zip: _____
Notes: _____

CONTACT 6
Name: _____ Email: _____
Phone # _____ Cell #: _____
Address: _____
City: _____ State: _____ Zip: _____
Notes: _____

Personal Contacts

CONTACT 7

Name: _____ Email: _____

Phone # _____ Cell #: _____

Address: _____

City: _____ State: _____ Zip: _____

Notes: _____

CONTACT 8

Name: _____ Email: _____

Phone # _____ Cell #: _____

Address: _____

City: _____ State: _____ Zip: _____

Notes: _____

CONTACT 9

Name: _____ Email: _____

Phone # _____ Cell #: _____

Address: _____

City: _____ State: _____ Zip: _____

Notes: _____

CONTACT 10

Name: _____ Email: _____

Phone # _____ Cell #: _____

Address: _____

City: _____ State: _____ Zip: _____

Notes: _____

CONTACT 11

Name: _____ Email: _____

Phone # _____ Cell #: _____

Address: _____

City: _____ State: _____ Zip: _____

Notes: _____

CONTACT 12

Name: _____ Email: _____

Phone # _____ Cell #: _____

Address: _____

City: _____ State: _____ Zip: _____

Notes: _____

Strategies & Activities For Your Self-Care

Here are some examples, and the list is not exhaustive, of coping strategies and activities that you can try. The key is to find a few things that engages you and provides a sense of accomplishment, relaxation, and/or peace, which can be a powerful tool for distraction and managing stress.

Baking	Home Decorating	Reading
Ballooning	Home Renovation	Rock Climbing
Beach Volleyball	Horseback Riding	Running
Biking	Jewelry Making	Scrapbooking
Bird Watching	Jigsaw Puzzles	Sewing
Board Games	Jogging	Singing
Bodyboarding	Journaling	Skiing
Building Blocks	Kayaking	Snowboarding
Building Toys	Knitting	Snowboarding
Calligraphy	Lampworking	Snowshoeing
Camping	Landscaping	Soap Carving
Candle Making	Learning A New Instrument	Soap Making
Canoeing	Learning A New Language	Stand Up Paddleboarding
Card Games	Legos	Stargazing
Coding	Meditation	Stretching
Coloring	Miniature Models Doll Houses	Surfing
Cooking	Miniature Modeling Train Sets	Taking A Bubble Bath
Crocheting	Mosaic	Video Editing
Crosswords	Mountain Biking	Video Games
Dancing	Nature Photography	Video Making
Deep Breathing	Needlepoint	Volunteer Work
Dinner Party	Origami	Walking
Dog Walking	Painting	Watching Documentaries
Drawing	Paper Mâché	Watching Movies
Embroidery	Pet Sitting	Weaving
Exercise	Photography	Weightlifting
Fishing	Picnicking	Wildlife Watching
Gardening	Playing An Instrument	Wood Carving
Geocaching	Playing Basketball	Woodworking
Glass Blowing	Playing Soccer	Word Searches
Glider Riding	Playing Tennis	Writing
Hand Lettering	Pottery	Yoga
Hiking	Quilting	Zumba

Here are just a few self-care and pampering ideas to help get you started

Acupuncture	Gourmet Coffee	Napping
Aromatherapy	Hiking	Nature
Attend A Workshop	Ice Cream	Pedicure
Bubble Bath	Make A Bucket List	Read
Calming Music	Make A Vision Board	Reiki
Deep Breathing	Manicure	Walking
Epsom Salt Soak	Massage	Watch A Funny Movie
Face Mask	Meditation	Yoga

More From Imaginate Publishing

FOR THE BOLD & BRAVE

90 Meetings In 90 Days Guided Aa Meeting Journal & Tracker
An AA's Little Handbook Of Hope Prayers Inspiration & Laughs
Get That Funky Monkey Off My Back! (Sweary Smoker's Trigger Tracker)
Five Minute Guided Trigger Tracker & Behavior Checker
Diary Of An Addict: 5 Minute Guided Trigger Tracker With Daily Journal
AA Powerful 12 Step Workbook With Trigger Tracker & Selfcare Check-Ins
AA 12 Step Workbook: Twelve Steps Journal To Sobriety
Stepping Through The First 90 Days: 12 Step Journal With Steps 10 - 12
Fourth Step Workbook: Aa Journal For Alcohol Recovery
Making Our 4-Column Grudge List: A 4th Step Inventory Workbook
Into Action: The Art Of Swapping Character Defects For Character Assets
Journaling Through The Next Six Months: 10th Step Journal
10th Step Inventory Journal: Step 10 Nightly Inventory
My 10th Step Inventory Journal - For Steps 10 & 11

IN A BELIEVER'S TOOLBOX

A Believer's Walk With Jesus: A Chronological Gospel Reading Plan & Journal
A Believer's Walk In Wisdom: 12 Flexible Bible Reading Plans & Journal
Journey Through The Bible: Chronological Bible Reading Plan & Journal
4-Month Bible Study Planner & Journal With Weekly Bible Verse
Inductive Bible Study Journal With 90 Guided Entries
Bible Study Journal: Drawing Closer To God (Soap Bible Study Prompts)
200 Page Notebook With Inspirational Quotes From The Bible
Gratitude Journal With Inspirational Quotes From The Bible
Undated Planner & Bible Study Journal: Making Time For God: 1 Year
Planner & Bible Study Journal (1 Year Dated - Blue or Orange)

JOURNALS FROM IMAGINATE

Making Love To My Demons: Shadow Work Guided Journal & Workbook
One Line A Day 5 Year Journal: The Story Of Me
From Russell Conwell's Acres Of Diamonds: A Success Journal
Cocktail Recipe Journal: Blank Cocktail & Mixed Drink Recipe Book
My Badass Cocktails: Blank Cocktail Recipe Book
My Badass Recipes: Blank Recipe Notebook Journal
100 Family Recipes Blank Recipe Journal
101 Recipes: Blank Recipe Notebook

Planners & Notebooks From Imaginate

SUCCESS IS PLANNED – PERSONAL PLANNERS

The Sophisticated Financial Budget Planner: Undated Monthly, Weekly, Daily
Undated Sunflowers & Butterflies Monthly & Weekly Planner
Undated Planner & Bible Study Journal: Making Time For God (12 months)
18 Month Midyear Academic Planner For April – September
12 Month Midyear Academic Planner For July – June
Planner & Bible Study Journal (1 Year Dated - Blue or Orange)
12 Month Dated Agenda With Weekly AA Slogans & Sobriety Tracker
12 Month Personal Planner: Monthly, Weekly & Daily - Pretty Purple Floral
12 Month Personal Planner: Monthly, Weekly & Daily
Two Year Monthly & Weekly Planner With Quotes
Two Year Monthly Planner With Quotes
Five Year Monthly Planner: 60 Month Agenda To Smash Your Goals

BEAUTIFULLY WATERMARKED DESIGNER NOTEBOOKS

Sunflowers & Butterflies: 120 Beautifully Watermarked Pages.
Silly Christmas Reindeer - 200 Pages College-Ruled or Wide-Ruled
Delightful Christmas Gnome - 200 Pages College-Ruled or Wide-Ruled
Magical Christmas Train - 200 Pages College-Ruled or Wide-Ruled
Shiny Christmas Tree - 200 Pages College-Ruled or Wide-Ruled
Cute Christmas Snowman - 200 Pages College-Ruled or Wide-Ruled
Falling Snow Flakes - 200 Pages College-Ruled or Wide-Ruled

VISIT THE BOLD & BRAVE	VISIT IMAGINATE PUBLISHING
www.addictionrecoverybooks.com	www.imaginateonline.com

Printed in Great Britain
by Amazon